To Roy Gib.

A fellow pilot in WWII

Mozart Kaufman

# fighter pilot

Aleutians to Normandy to Stalag Luft I

# fighter pilot
## Aleutians to Normandy to Stalag Luft I

Mozart Kaufman

M & A Kaufman Publishers

M & A Kaufman Publishers
2 Magnolia Avenue
San Anselmo, California 94960


Book design and production by Fisher-Dizick,
Corte Madera, California

Cover design by Phillip Dizick

Typesetting by Deborah Fisher

Edited by Mary Leydecker & Annette Kaufman

Printed and bound by BookCrafters, Chelsea, Michigan


ISBN 0-9636301-0-5

10  9  8  7  6  5  4  3  2  1

Printed in the United States of America

To my wife, Annette,
who changed my life after we married in 1967.

It was she who gave me the idea of carrying antiques in my
retail store, and it was this suggestion that led to 17
wonderful years of travel to England, France and Italy to
buy beautiful antiques. While buying in Normandy, we
found the location of my fighter base at Deux-Jumeaux,
where the only thing left was the steel webbing used by
farmers for fencing. Then in England, we found my air
strip at Ibsley, where buildings remained but in a state of
disrepair.

In 1978, my wife was instrumental in my finding a
wonderful art teacher, who made me into a passable artist.

In 1989, with her encouragement I started this book.
This is the result.

# Acknowledgments

The writing of this book was interrupted when in 1990 I suffered a stroke. With encouragement and help from my wife Annette I was able to continue writing it. After many corrections and revisions it was finally completed.

My friends and wartime buddies helped me fill in the voids. Thanks to Victor N. Cabas, Richard Morrissey, Edward J. Zienka (deceased), Woody R. Klinner Jr. (deceased), Max L. Campbell, Paul W. Robinson, William R. Johnson (deceased), Jesse D. Lefforge, Leo Greenfield, Richard C. Williams, Walter F. Dudek, Kenneth A. Sadick, Richard W. Lederman, Coleman Jacobson, Paul E. Farber, Raymond F. Toliver (author), and Hanns Scharff.

My gratitude also to Mary Leydecker for her patience with the many phone calls while she edited the book, and to Phillip Dizick and Deborah Fisher for their expertise in putting the book together and their friendship and understanding above and beyond the call of duty.

Please forgive the misspelled or omitted names – 50 years is a long time to remember.

.

# Contents

# Prologue

I came in blazing with my guns wide open and dropped my bomb right under the tread of the tank. There was no way he could get away this time. At the same moment as I fired my guns and dropped my bomb, bullets hit my plane. I couldn't have been more than 10 feet off the ground as I went over the tank when my engine burst into flames and the plane became a flying torch.

Behind the tank on the road was a hill, and I pulled my stick back to gain altitude. I realized I had to get out of the plane fast. The flames were a solid mass around me but were kept out of the cockpit by the closed canopy. At about 500 feet, I opened my canopy and with that, the flames swept in and almost enveloped me. I pushed up to get out and then realized I hadn't released my safety belt. I ducked down out of the flames, released the belt and pushed out. As I got out on the right side, flames began to lick at me. I went through intense heat, fanned by oil from the engine. But there was no time for fear, no time for hesitation, only time for action. The second I was clear of the plane I pulled my rip cord and felt a jerk. I didn't have time to look to see if my chute had opened before my feet hit the ground.

I immediately had a few quick thoughts about making escape plans, and I unbuckled my parachute and looked around for a direction to run.

When I started up the hill, a German soldier came running down toward me with a drawn Luger pistol.

More than four decades later, Mozart Kaufman still can recall vividly his last mission as a fighter-bomber pilot over France during World War II, his capture, interrogation and solitary confinement by the Luftwaffe and the hardships of life in an East German prison camp, where the last months were spent segregated with other Jewish-American pilots who had been told they were to be exterminated.

At home in front of some of my oil paintings.
Photograph by Art Rogers, Point Reyes, California

# 1

## A Future Pilot—Growing Up

From my earliest childhood, this country's wars were an integral part of my life.

My boyhood hometown of Vicksburg, Miss. sits on a bluff facing the river, surrounded on three sides by a national military park, the original battlefield site of the Siege of Vicksburg, acres of tableaux frozen in time. The gun emplacements and trenches still stand as mute reminders of the devastating struggle to defend the city against Union forces until the surrender on July 4, 1863. The surrender gave General Ulysses S. Grant's forces control of the Mississippi River and divided the South from the Southwest.

It was 54 years later on June 9, 1917, that I was born in this city, where for decades Independence Day was not celebrated. It was not until July 4, 1952, when President Eisenhower visited Vicksburg that the people began displaying flags and having celebrations.

I grew up in this park, this memorial to the Confederacy loss. It was my playground. Its monuments built by both the northern and southern states in memory of their fallen dead, these monuments were my haunts. I was a typical southern boy reared in a sleepy town with the past all around me. The National Cemetery within the park was the burial place of the northern troops, and it was a sad place to visit, but a beautiful resting place for the 17,000 soldiers and sailors who had died in the battle trying to preserve the Union.

I had a carefree life, roaming the park from one end to the other, feeling the majesty of those great monuments. The Illinois monument was one I especially liked. It was huge and stately, a white marble building, modeled after the Pantheon in Rome. Walking up the impressive stone stairway and entering the doorway, a shaft of sunlight poured down from a large opening in the ceiling. Around the marble walls were 60 bronze tablets with more than 36,000 names of soldiers from Illinois who had fought in the great siege. Even as a small boy, I felt the grandeur, like going into a sacred place.

In our little town, Sunday picnics were a way of life, with several families getting together and driving out to the monuments. There we sat on benches and shared picnic lunches, and my big treat was the fried chicken and wedges of cold watermelon.

Even though I was a Southerner, my favorite monument was the large statue of Gen. Ulysses S. Grant sitting astride a horse on a high stone pedestal. Much to my mother's disapproval, I loved to climb on it. I could barely reach the top of the pedestal to pull myself up, and then by stretching, I could reach his boot in the stirrup.

I would then shinny up his leg and finally climb to the top and sit with my legs wrapped around the crown of the general's hat. The crown of his hat was as large as my whole body, and I remember thinking he must be 30 to 40 feet high, but much later I found out the monument was only 19 feet tall.

This was before I thought of being a fighter pilot.

My best friends were the sons of a neighbor, Major John C. H. Lee: John Jr. and Gwin Robbins and I did everything small boys do to have fun in a small town – sandlot baseball, fishing for crawfish in the creek that ran through our neighborhood and climbing the tallest trees. When the Chautauqua, a black minstrel show, came to town, I did odd jobs to earn free passes, and this in my eyes was the biggest artistic event in Vicksburg.

A short distance from my home was a large pecan grove. Although we had three pecan trees in my own yard, we boys would go to the grove to steal the nuts. We knew the caretaker had a shotgun and he said he would shoot us and put us in the large gunny sack in which he collected nuts if he caught us, but we picked nuts anyway. We called the caretaker "Sack-to-Billy."

When I grew up, I never took up smoking, but when I was very young, I gave it a try. We used dried corn silk and newspapers to make cigarettes. I coughed and sputtered, discovering soon enough that smoking was not for me.

Roller skating hockey was the big sport. I remember I would cut the straightest limb from an oak tree with a curve at the bottom for a hockey stick and we used a tin can for a puck. We played on a paved street and very soon into the game the tin can was a solid sharp lethal missile.

Baseball was always a favorite too, but the real fun baseball game was played with a broomstick and bottle tops. To play this game, the pitcher sailed bottle caps to the batter and the bases run depended upon how far you hit the bottle cap.

John Lee's father was in the United States Army Engineers, stationed in Vicksburg with the flood control division for the Mississippi River.

One winter we had one of our rare snowstorms in Vicksburg and ended up with several inches of snow. Major Lee had a beautiful sleigh which he tied to the bumper of his car. John, Gwin, and I sat on the sleigh together and were pulled all over the town. We came home soaking and cold but happy and exhilarated.

3

Finally Major Lee's term of duty was up and he had to move on. As a final farewell, he took John Jr. and all of his friends on the Army paddle-wheel boat for an overnight cruise on the Mississippi River. We slept in cabins on real bunks, ate wonderful food and had a great time. At the end of the voyage we said goodbye to our good friend John. That was in the 1920s. I didn't hear about the family again until I was in Normandy in July 1944. That's when I learned that "Major" Lee was the general in command of logistics to supply all materiel and supplies that moved to the continent for the Normandy invasion. I then read that Colonel John C.H. Lee Jr., my friend, had been captured by the Germans right after the invasion, escaped and returned to his outfit.

I was the youngest of four children, and from an early age my brother and two sisters were responsible for my education. My brother, Philip, and sisters, Caroline and Phyllis, inherited all of their brains and intellect from my mother. But when I was born, Mother had given all that wonderful intellect and brains to her first three children and there was none left for me. I was born with a love of life but not much love for school. My brother and sisters were exasperated with my lack of interest in academics and were constantly coaching me so that I could continue on to the next grade with my classmates. Teachers were always so glad to see me enter their class at the beginning of the term. They thought, "another bright Kaufman." They learned soon enough that I was not the studious pupil they had expected. There were just too many big trees to climb and too many pecans to steal.

Boy Scouting was a very important part of my life. I became an Eagle Scout, but when a Sea Scout unit was formed in our town, I was one of the first to join. Mr. A.M. Burrows was the Sea Scout master, and he was a dedicated man who instilled in me all the important things I should know about being a good and honest citizen in the community.

One of the first things he did was to secure an old boat from the Navy. It was a boat that had been used to move men from ship to shore. It was in terrible condition, but Mr. Burrows had it put on a railroad flat car and moved into the workshop of the railroad where he worked. He and his fellow workers got busy and in their spare time put the boat into ship-shape condition.

It was a very exciting day when we launched that boat. We took overnight cruises up the Yazoo River. We would set up a camp site and take our small row boat out at midnight for frog hunting. With a flashlight and a three-prong gig on a pole we would search the riverbank for frogs. We would put our catch into a gunny sack and the next morning we would cook up a mess of frog legs over the campfire.

When I was 13 years old, I lost my father. My memories of my father are somehow connected with the bakery he had opened when I was seven. My father was 41 years old when I was born. Life was different in those days. A man was an "older person" when he was in his 40s. My dad did not throw baseballs to me or play any other active sport with me. Whether it was age or just his personality, I don't know. I'm sure I must have been overwhelming to him with my natural exuberance. I still have some of his collection of classical records on the old 78s – Caruso, Galli-Curci and more. But the memories I have were my times with him in our bakery. I would go over to the bakery after school and he would let me eat all the cookies and cakes I wanted. I never remember my Daddy depriving me of eating any of the bakery goods, but he always reminded me to eat the broken and unattractive goods rather than the most salable. He always said, "You can't eat the whole thing at once anyway." One thing I really liked was when he would let me wait on customers. I would bag what they wanted and take the money to the regular clerk to ring up and she would give me the change for the customer. I was a born merchant and didn't realize it.

Our family owned a farm right outside of town. We rented it to a sharecropper and as I remember, it made a very poor living for him. I loved going out with Daddy to visit the farm. He would talk to the farmer while I chased the chickens and played with the pigs and cows. On the way home through the battlefield park, we would go walking over the hills and the battlements and he would repeat the stories of the Vicksburg siege. These were my best memories of my father.

My mother was a typical Southern lady. Up until the time Daddy died in 1930, Mother led a very genteel life, raising her children, sewing dresses for her girls and planning the meals for the day with Rachel, our cook and housekeeper. But when my father died, she had to work and run the bakery. By 1934, my brother and sisters were off to college at Louisiana State University in Baton Rouge. This was during the Great Depression and the cost of those three going to college away from home plus the expense of keeping up the home in Vicksburg was more than Mother could handle. We decided to sell the bakery and move to New York, where we could live in an apartment while the older three attended Columbia University. So the five of us piled into the old Chandler car and set off for New York City. We drove across the South, stopping off in Birmingham, Ala., to visit family and then to Washington, D.C., to see our nation's capital for the first time. It was the most beautiful city I had ever seen – white marble buildings from one end to the other. Then on to New York City, which we entered through the Holland Tunnel. What a disappointment! It was so big and dirty, full of people rushing everywhere, and I realized that my carefree days in Vicksburg were gone. This was a new chapter in my life.

The first thing I did was to join the Sea Scouts to pick up where I had left off. What a culture shock it was to meet those brash rough New Yorkers. It didn't take me long to leave scouting. Since I had no friends in New York, I began taking an interest in school. The results were very satisfying and it was a pleasure to see A's and B's on my report card.

The summer before my senior year, I wanted to fill in the

time so I signed up for a month of training with the C.M.T.C. (Citizens Military Training Camp) and went off to Camp Dix, New Jersey. It turned out to be a hard month of soldiering and being thrown in with some of the most foul-mouthed unsavory characters. That month of June in 1935 certainly took the innocence out of the small-town boy from Vicksburg. At the end of this training period we marched out to a training field for graduation. There were at least a thousand men. We spread out our gear to pitch our tents. We were told to break ranks, pitch our tent, pack our gear and stand at attention. I was the first on the field to complete the exercise, and the sergeant pointed to me and yelled out "number one." This one episode changed my life. From that moment on, I had gained the confidence I needed and I felt I was as good as any man alive.

After graduating from high school, I had no further interest in schooling. I left home and went to Little Rock, Ark., to work for my uncle, Sam Grundfest, who owned Sterling Stores, a chain of variety and small department stores in the South. I liked the work and it turned out to be the direction I would head in life. I also liked Little Rock. I made my best friends there and even though I was far from my own family, I felt more at home there than I did in Vicksburg or New York. But this pleasant life was not to last.

We were hearing and reading about the troubles in Europe and it all sounded ominous. German refugees had moved into my community and they told how they had to flee their country and leave all their possessions behind. The stories of the terrible oppression and suffering were unbelievable.

Hitler was flexing his muscles and Neville Chamberlain was trying to keep peace at any cost.

However, his attempts were to no avail and in September 1939, Hitler's troops and Stuka bombers roared into Poland. World War II had begun with a ferocity that was unparalleled in our time. At home, in America, the feelings were cautious and grave concern, but we had the Atlantic Ocean between us and we felt reasonably safe.

My career was moving along at a nice pace, and I felt I had a good chance for advancement. But by 1940, my concern about what was happening in the world became overwhelming. When the Nazis swept through Europe from Norway, through France and took Paris on June 14, 1940, the Atlantic Ocean had shrunk to the size of a big pond for me. With the draft hanging over my head, I decided not to wait much longer to get my service completed. On October 15, 1940, I signed up for one year.

# 2

# I Knew I Wanted to Fly

I was sent to Fort Leavenworth, Kansas, and the first six weeks I was back in basic training for the second time; however, I enjoyed the hard exercise and getting into shape.

Shortly after I arrived, the draft did begin and men started pouring into Fort Leavenworth for their first processing. I knew that when I finished basic training, I would have to make a decision about which branch of the Army I wanted to apply for.

During a question and answer period, I was asked if I knew how to type. I was a slow ten-finger typist, but I answered yes. This was the hardest lesson I learned throughout the war. Never again, until I finally left the service at the end of 1945, did I tell the truth and admit I could type. Because of this admission I lost any chance to pick a branch of the service that I preferred and was assigned to the Quartermaster Corps because I had been in the retail business. At this post, I handed out clothes to new recruits for the balance of the year. This was certainly not the height of my military career.

However, after three months I was promoted to corporal and given a raise to $75 a month. This promotion was more of a thrill than any other I received throughout the war. At the end of my service on October 15, 1941, I went back to my job in Little Rock. In December I was managing one of the stores in Tullahoma, Tenn., relieving a store manager temporarily. On Sunday morning, December 7, 1941, I went to work to get the store ready for the

Christmas business. At 7 p.m. I finally finished working and went out for dinner. That's when I heard about Pearl Harbor and realized there would be no more peace for Americans for a long time.

The next day I phoned the Sterling Stores headquarters and turned in my resignation effective December 24, and on Christmas Day I was on my way to New York, to visit my mother before joining up again. While in New York, I was trying to decide what to do. The Army Air Corps was my first choice, and I almost signed up then and there, but I remembered my summer at C.M.T.C, and I had no desire to go through training again with guys from the New York area; so I decided to wait until I got back to Little Rock.

In 1940 I was a private at Fort Leavenworth, Kansas.

As soon as I returned, I reported to the induction center. Having had no college education and wanting to be a pilot, I was given an appointment to report for a special exam that would qualify me for air cadet training. I passed and was sworn in as an aviation cadet on January 24, 1942.

I was sent to Williams Field, Arizona, for a month of – you guessed it – basic training. Since we were cadets, it was called pre-flight training. However, whatever it was called, this was my third and I hoped my final basic training.

By the end of February, we had had our fill of marching all day long in the desert and were more than ready for flying school training. They sent us to a place called Cal Aero Academy in Ontario, California. Cal Aero was like a country club compared to Williams Field. We called it "Major Mosely's School for Boys."

The flying instructors were civilians. They wore officer's uniforms and silver wings but had no rank and were addressed as "Mister," but we lived in fear of these men because they held our military future in their hands. I'm sure they all received commissions as officers shortly after we left.

On February 5, I walked out onto the field, and there was the biggest and most beautiful airplane I had ever seen. This was

a Stearman Primary PT-13B trainer with a powerful 225-horsepower Lycoming engine. This was what I had been waiting for and I was thrilled. Mr. Tangerman was my instructor, and I knew he would either teach me to fly or wash me out and send me to hell – the infantry. I climbed up to the front seat with Mr. Tangerman behind me, and we took off and flew for 22 minutes, closer to heaven than I had ever been. There followed days of long-winded instructions and some crazy flying. One month later, March 28, with 15 flying hours behind me, I took off for a routine lesson. I was still try-

My first plane, a Stearman PT 13-B with a powerful 225 HP Lycoming engine.

ing to make a perfect landing. I will never know what happened, but the landing was not only bad, it was frightening as hell.

Mr. Tangerman grabbed the controls and saved us from a catastrophe. We landed in one piece, but I was sure he was going

Primary Training with Cadets Peter Landis, Johnny Mize, William D. Packard and myself with Mr. Tangerman our Civilian Flight Instructor, Cal Aero Academy, CA. Johnny Mize had just left the St. Louis Browns to join up. He returned to baseball after the war to become a big leaguer.

to boot me out. So many other fellows had been washed out after incidents like this during the past month. He climbed out fast, and as I started to unbuckle, he said, "OK, take it off – it's all yours." I found it hard to believe, and the only thing I could think was that he was too scared to go up with me again.

Filled with excitement, I taxied out and took off into the so-called "wild blue yonder." When I reached 3,000 feet, I began to soar, free as a bird, diving, twisting and turning. It's a feeling one can have in a plane only once in a life time. After 32 minutes in heaven, I came in for my smoothest three-point landing yet, just as if I'd been doing it every time.

I knew then I wanted to be a fighter pilot, I wanted to fly alone in a single-engine plane, answering to no one and controlling my own destiny.

As the days and weeks went by, I learned to do loops, chandelles and split S's, turning the plane on its back and pulling through on a screaming dive toward the ground before pulling up.

A routine test was for the instructor to pull the throttle from my hand as he chopped the power, testing me for a "dead-stick" landing. Frantically, I would search the countryside – citrus trees as far as the eye could see, broken by low hills and houses – with

2,000 to 3,000 feet to glide down and find an emergency landing spot, finally spotting a small place that might work. "Check which way the wind is blowing. Search for smoke from a chimney. Look at the way trees are swaying and head down." At the last minute, the instructor would push the throttle forward and we'd begin to climb for another test.

One of the first solo accidents occurred when Cadet Kenneth Snow came in for a landing and his plane flipped upside down with Snow hanging from his seat belt. We all dashed out to help him out of the plane, but before we could reach him, he unbuckled his seat belt and fell to the ground, landing on his head. Luckily he had a hard head and was back flying in short order.

By the end of April we had graduated but we remained at Cal Aero Academy for basic flight training. We had seen many of our fellow cadets washed out by then, but there was much more to come in the months ahead. All of our planes were flown out and new planes flown in. I had thought the PT-13 with its wonderful open cockpit was the greatest, but here was a sleek plane with a closed cockpit, a BT-15 Vultee with a powerful 450-horsepower Wright engine. This was a big one and I looked forward to the challenge. Mr. Colbach was my new instructor, a very handsome blond fellow who seemed much easier then Mr. Tangerman...maybe it was because I wasn't pulling so many dumb

In Basic Training, Cadets Don L. Kimber, Oral W. Lee, Joseph P. Landis and myself with Mr. Colbach, Civilian Flight Instructor, Cal Aero Academy, CA.

things by this time or maybe it was because he didn't have to fly with me as often.

Almost a month later, we were flying formations cross-country and learning to fly on instruments. We also had many hours in the Link Trainer, an airplane sitting in a room. It had no wings, no tail, no engine or landing gear. It was the meanest, most cantankerous contraption that was ever developed. As I sat in this "box," there was a cockpit complete in every detail facing me, but no way to see out. The fiend sitting at the controls outside had the ability to simulate any kind of weather condition you could imagine and, of course, I would have to use the instruments to fly through these conditions. The guy at the controls was brutal, but we learned to cope with weather.

I moved up to Basic Training, a Vultee BT-15, 450 HP Wright engine.

The most exciting thing was the plan for night flying. A group of us flew down to Rosamund Dry Lake, a flying field in the desert. As I remember, the field was marked off, but we could also land elsewhere for miles around. We were given instructions on night flying and after a few days of acclimation with the area, I was told that tonight was "it" for me. There was a beautiful sunset and then dusk turned into a very dark night. I remember feeling a sense of excitement and apprehension as I sat in my plane at

At Rosamond Dry Lake this was the only way to take a bath at this desert strip.

the end of the runway, ready to take off – nothing but a black void ahead of me. I pushed the throttle forward and before I knew it, I was up in the most fantastic and beautiful atmosphere – thousands of brilliant stars bouncing off the nose of my place and the black desert below with an occasional lighted farm house. I took a deep breath and felt my excitement subsiding into a feeling of peace and contentment. I could have floated up there for hours.

(Forty years later I heard Pappy Boyington, the famous Flying Tiger pilot, speak to a group of 500 Rotarians at a fly-in gathering. During a question and answer period, he was asked about the most exciting moment in his flying career.

I turned to friends and said, "His first night flight," and sure enough, that was his answer.)

After graduation I went to Luke Field, Arizona, for advanced flight training. This again meant a course in handling a bigger plane. The AT-6A was the last step before fighter planes. The first couple of weeks I flew with my instructor, but from then until graduation, I was flying solo.

Towards the end of August, I was sent to Victorville, California, to check out in the AT-9, the twin-engine trainer. I was really disheartened as this was a kiss of death for a cadet wanting to fly fighter planes, but after four days of flying twin-engine, I returned to Luke Field.

Finally, graduation came, and we all waited impatiently for

the list to be posted to see who would fly fighters and who would fly bombers. I thought most of the men wanted to fly fighters, but I was amazed at how many applied to be bomber pilots.

I was lucky. I not only drew fighters, but I was assigned to Hamilton Field in Marin County, California, right across the new Golden Gate Bridge from the beautiful city of San Francisco. This turned out to be a prophetic move for me, as I ended up in Marin County after the war, married and raising a family of four children.

But back to graduation day. I put on my green dress coat with pink slacks, the silver wings on my chest and gold bars for my shoulders. But the best thing I had was a chance to be a fighter pilot, and I was ready.

# 3

# My First Fighter Plane

The Class of 42H, 250 strong, were given orders that scattered them all over the country, with 36 of us headed for Hamilton Field. There we settled in at the bachelor officer quarters for some heavy concentration on the new plane we would fly.

When we reported on the flight line to see our Airacobra P39 D-1 Warbird fighter plane, it was more than we could have hoped for. This plane was small, but it was a compact power house, built with not only .50-caliber guns but also a 37-millimeter cannon in the nose. The cockpit was entered by a door from the wing into the smallest possible space.

Flying this plane was like being in a powerful hornet.

The first week we spent learning everything we could about this fighter, both in the cockpit and in the books. The instrument panel, levers and handles were studied so thoroughly that we were ready for a blindfold test, and with our eyes covered, we could put our hands on every instrument, lever, and handle. This was imperative so we could take a quick glance at an instrument whether we were flying close formation on instruments in a storm or in combat.

I was ready.

On September 9. I took my first flight without an instructor, and it was an exciting moment to take off in such a powerful plane without help in a back seat. When I pushed the throttle forward, racing down the runway and lifting effortlessly into the sky, it was a whole new experience.

From here we worked on formations, and I mean close, really close formations with wings tucked in with the leader. It was not considered too close unless we scraped paint. This was the real fun of flying.

Landing was a great challenge to bring a single plane or a flight of four screaming down at full speed on the deck towards the end of the runway, chopping the throttle all the way back, pulling up in a perfect 360-degree circle and landing without touching the throttle again. This was training for fast landing in

Here we learned to fly a tight formation in the P39.

combat when returning from a mission when the planes were low on gasoline.

Meanwhile, my mother, who had spent little time with me in the seven years since I had left New York for Little Rock, decided to come visit me before I was sent overseas. She arrived in mid-September and almost immediately began "match-making." In a devious, motherly way, she found one of the leading families in Marin with a young, eligible daughter. Before I knew it, we were visiting the Harry Albert family and their daughter, Lois. After a whirlwind courtship, Lois and I were married a month and a half later on October 22, 1942.

One day the captain called for a volunteer to fly an officer in a small plane to Fresno in the central part of the state, drop him off and return the same day. The chance to fly a different type of plane halfway across California was irresistible.

I gathered maps together and went down to the flight line for a check-out with the crew chief. The plane turned out to be a small Taylorcraft 65-horsepower Cub plane, and although I don't remember the details, there were so few things to learn that it was all over in two or three minute – altimeter, compass, turn and bank, take off at 40 mph, cruise to 60 mph, and that was about it.

I took off and headed south, carefully watching my map and observing each town as it went by. It was slow going, but I finally

Another photo of the same four planes. Only props and tails of other planes can be seen.

got to Fresno, dropped off my passenger, had a sandwich, gassed up and headed home. I don't know what happened – maybe I had a strong head wind, but I didn't have the slightest idea where I was. I was flying over hills and forests and if I did see a town, it was so small I couldn't identify it from the map.

The only thing I could do was to stay on my planned compass heading. But the problem was that after flying a P-39 at 225 to 250 mph, I was used to seeing the ground go by and check points show up so much more rapidly. In this plane, even if I had picked up a 25-mile head wind, I was only making 35 mph. I thought to myself that I could do better with a good horse, but my sarcasm didn't help me find out where I was. It seemed like hours were going by and I even thought my watch was broken. In desperation,

I changed my heading to go westward towards the Pacific Ocean. This way I could follow the coastline north to San Francisco, and I knew that sooner or later I would find my base.

I breathed a sigh of relief when I saw civilization below, and recognized San Jose in the south end of the San Francisco Bay. Then I realized my gas was low because I had been crawling along like a snail. As I neared Mills Field (now the San Francisco International Airport), I knew I had to decide to land and get gas or to sweat it out and make it home. I kept going and as I passed the Golden Gate Bridge, my gauge now read zero. God, the plane was crawling and to make matters worse, the sun had set and dusk was spreading over the sky.

In the distance, I saw Hamilton Field and I prayed they would turn the lights on for me. As I finally landed, the last of the fuel was gone. The crew chief met me and checked the gauge and said, "You don't have ANY gas."

During the middle of October I started doing easy aerobatics, but we were all concerned about the troubles being experienced with the P-39. Some of the pilots talked about the plane "tumbling" when it was in the middle of aerobatics and spins, but no one could pin down what was wrong. Since I had arrived at Hamilton Field, we had lost four pilots in P-39s.

By now I had 58 hours flying time in the P-39 and was scheduled to go up on an aerobatics mission and practice stalls and spins for the first time in this plane. I hadn't done spins and stalls since June because the AT-6 that I flew in training at Luke Field was considered unsafe to practice those maneuvers.

On October 27, we lost our fifth pilot, my friend Lt. John Niosi from my 42H class. We had no answer as to the cause. There was no radio communication from John to give us any hint that he had been in trouble – just another crash without warning.

On the evening of October 30, my wife and I had invited a buddy pilot over for a visit and we discussed the troubles we were having with our planes. I told him that I was scheduled to fly the next morning and to do spins and stalls for the first time. I said, "There is no way I'm going to go into the ground with that damn plane."

I have always been the type of person who thinks ahead about emergencies that might face me. When I'm driving along a two-lane road with cars coming towards me, I automatically think what I would do if an oncoming car were to cross over into my lane. I was doing the same thing with this airplane, looking ahead to a possible emergency.

I had love for this P-39. It was the first fighter plane that I flew after graduation from flying school, but this plane was a killer. I had a feeling of love/hate filled with respect for what it could do to me.

At 8:00 the next morning I took off in my P-39. It was a clear day, perfect for this mission. Beautiful Mount Tamalpais was to my right, and San Francisco was connected to Marin County by a ribbon of steel, the Golden Gate Bridge. The sparkling blue waters of the bay spread out to the north, one of the most beautiful bays in the world. But the beauty was not on my mind this morning. I had before me the most serious mission of my life.

I climbed slowly to 13,000 feet, a safe altitude for my maneuver, and I pulled up into a stall to get the feel of the plane as it shuddered and began to lose lift. I had a funny feeling that I wanted more altitude between me and the ground, so I climbed to 15,000 feet and did a power-off spin without a problem. Next I planned to do a power-on spin to the left. I raised the nose of the plane much higher, keeping the throttle open until I felt the plane begin to mush and shudder and fall over to the left in a power-on spin.

Speed built up fast as I hurtled in a twisting turn and immediately applied full opposite rudder followed by stick forward and aileron to the left to recover out of the spin. Nothing happened. The plane wasn't responding and was going into a very vicious spin. I tried my rudder and stick again, but the plane continued hurtling down at a twisting, frightening speed. I tried again and then realized it was time to get out. The rate of the descent speed was eating up the altitude too fast for me.

I released my safety belt, pulled the release handle on the right hand door and gave it a firm yank. Nothing happened. I tried again and then threw my shoulder against the door. Again, I tried to no avail. Then I reached for the left door emergency handle, pulled hard and threw my shoulder against the door again and again. I turned back to the right door. I was going down in a flying coffin, and the cold waters of the bay were getting closer by the second. With adrenalin pounding through my body, I pulled the handle and with superhuman strength, I slammed my shoulder against the door and felt it leave my hand and fly off into space.

The entire time of the dive I had been thrown around like a ball. Leaning out, I felt the wind like a hurricane snatching me out over the wing. The tail was flailing around behind me and my thought was, "God help me if I hit that thing." I waited a few seconds, and when I was free and clear, I reached for the parachute ripcord and gave it a firm pull. I felt a tug and looked up to see that beautiful white silk parachute blossoming over my head. I swung lazily back and forth, settling down towards the waters of San Pablo Bay. Meanwhile, my plane was continuing down in its mad twisting turn until it splashed with a tremendous explosion below. I had fallen 9,000 to 12,000 feet and I felt luck was with me. I gave a tug to the shrouds of my chute and I hit the water. The chute billowed out on the water. I gathered it together in my arms and began looking around. I saw boats in the distance, and I knew there was nothing to be concerned about – I would be picked up soon.

It wasn't long before a sport fisherman arrived to pull me from the water and we headed for Hamilton Field.

Meanwhile, a flat-bottomed boat driven by airplane-type propellers was coming at top speed across the shallow marsh land from Hamilton Field to pick me up. This was the end of October, and the cold water and high speed made my clothes feel like ice, but I was alive and that's all I cared about. I had beaten the odds and I was the first to live to tell about it.

I was rushed to the hospital for a good hot shower and then put to bed for 24 hours of rest and observation. My first request was to call my wife and let her know what had happened and to tell her not to worry. An orderly told me there was no phone handy and that he had received orders I was to stay in bed. However, he agreed to make the call for me and I lay back to wait for my wife to come visit me.

By noon I still had not heard from her, but my first visitor came at 12:30 p.m. – it was my father-in-law, Harry Albert. "How in the hell did you find out about this?" I asked him. Harry Albert, a well-known merchant in Marin and a leading citizen of San Rafael, said he had received a phone call from the local newspaper, the Independent Journal. He was asked if Mozart Kaufman was his son-in-law and then told about my having bailed out. It was only a week earlier that the newspaper had published a report of my marriage to Harry Albert's daughter.

I decided I would not let my mother in New York know about this incident. Ironically, Mother had warned me to be careful and her advice was to "fly low and slow." But the very next day I received a frantic call from my mother, who had learned about the accident from the New York Times, which had carried a story about me on the front page.

Three days later I was flying again in formation with my buddies. I had thought there would be a funny feeling as I raced down the runway to take off, but it was just another flight.

A few days later I was called before a hearing board to report what had happened in my flight, why I had failed to recover from the spin. I felt as if the board, which included my group commander, Major Frederick Granbo, was trying to pick every corner of my brain to get the answers. Finally, I was asked if I had pulled the throttle when I went into the power-on spin. I told them that there were written instructions on the bulletin board and there was nothing about pulling the throttle in a spin.

Learning this, Major Granbo went up the next day to find out if this was the problem. We all stood around watching him take off and waiting for him to return from the flight. After five lives had been lost, I was the first pilot in our group to bail out and live to give us any hope for an answer.

When Major Granbo landed, we all gathered around him to hear his report. He said he had climbed to 17,000 feet and gone into a power-on spin. He told us this was the most violent flight he had ever been in, and there was no way he could recover from the spin with the power on. But when he pulled the throttle all the way back, the plane slowed to a normal spin and he was able to recover without any problem.

Forty-five years later I wrote to the Air Force for a microfilm copy of the test and this was what I received:

"The pilot was on an aerobatic mission, practicing spins. He had done some right hand spins and tried one to the left. Pilot failed to bring the plane out of the left hand spin and at 6,000 feet the pilot bailed out of the plane.

Subject:    Spin Tests P-39-D-1, Nov 10/42

LEFT HAND SPIN

Start 14,000 feet – recovered at 6,500 feet. Number of turns before attempted recover: 3 Three turns after application of recovery methods with no indication of recovery. Recovered in about one turn, after complete turn with throttle closed and use of normal recovery technique.Spin was fairly steady and a tendency to be flat (approximately 20 to 30 degrees nose down from the horizon). During the flat part of the spin (throttle on) it required both hands to get the stick forward.

Subject:  Spin Tests P-39-D-1, Nov 10/42

Note:  A.  Loss of altitude in all tests includes the recovery dive.

B.  Further tests with "power on" were contemplated, but it is believed to be definitely dangerous type of spin and so unnerving that the tests were concluded after the 3rd power on spin.

Conclusions:

A.  Controls leading up to spin:

1.  Throttle off!

2.  Propeller low rpm.

3.  Controls with spin until recovery is desired.

B.  Recovery:

1.  Full opposite rudder during slow portion of spin oscillation.

2.  Stick forward and ailerons against the spin after rudder has begun to have effect.

Note:  Throttle off during recovery until in straight dive and then normal flight operation."

In 1991 I wrote to a man who had graduated with me at Luke Field in Arizona and who had gone on with me to Hamilton Field in September 1942, asking him if he had any information about the loss of P-39 pilots at Hamilton Field.

Frederick Hagerman's reply to me was this: "In October I went up with another pilot to practice stalls, spins, etc. As I recall, we did a split 'S' over the bay. I recovered but the other pilot went into the bay and did not get out."

In 1989 I received a video tape of the P-39 Warbird checkout introduction. In viewing the movie, I found that the greatest improvement over my P-39D model was the installation of a large emergency release handle for the right hand door. Instructions said, "Reduce speed for emergency release of the door." Pulling this handle released the hinges and the door fell completely away from the plane. In the P-39D that I had bailed out of, we only had the regular handle with which to open the door and there was no warning about slowing the speed of the plane before bailing out. It took the loss of many lives to solve the problems with this plane after it was first produced. In my case, I not only saved my own life but also helped save many pilots in the future.

# 4

## Missions over the Aleutians

A month later, November 21, a group of us received orders to proceed to Seattle, Wash., and on to Elmendorf Field, Anchorage, Alaska. Alaska was the stepping-off point for the Aleutian chain, the front line to keep the Japanese from taking Alaska and then advancing down the coast to California.

(On June 3, 1942, just six months after the attack on Pearl Harbor, Japanese planes had bombed the naval and air base on the island of Unalaska at Dutch Harbor. This was followed by another attack on June 4. Seventy-seven American servicemen were killed.

A week later on June 13 the Japanese had moved in with naval forces and captured Kiska and Attu, taking 11 American servicemen manning the weather station at Kiska.

Two days later, when the weather cleared up, U. S. forces moved in and sank one cruiser and severely damaged three other cruisers, an aircraft carrier, a destroyer and a gunboat. With the capture of these two islands, the Japanese had a foothold in the west that we would have to fight for the next 12 months.)

The ultimate destination for us would be the far end of the Aleutian Chain (see page 36). Here we were flying for the first time in snow and all-weather conditions. The P-40 Warhawk Tomahawk, the old workhorse of fighter planes, would be our plane in this theater of operations.

This fighter plane, which went back long before the December 7 attack on Pearl Harbor, was proven by General Chennault and his Flying Tigers to be better than the Japanese Zero, and then went on to lick the best German fighters in Russia, North Africa, and Europe before the P-47 and P-51 came on line to carry us to victory in 1945.

It was on the first morning when I climbed into the cockpit that I saw a shiny, new brass plate warning pilots "when in a spin, pull the throttle." I realized that my harrowing experience at Hamilton Field had not been for naught.

At this time in early 1943, the Japanese were on the island of Kiska and had a small air field and submarine pen there. Farther out they also controlled the island of Attu with many troops. But the real danger was the Japanese fleet, which was roaming the Pacific Ocean and reaching out to the Aleutians to supply their bases on the two islands they held. We expected a Japanese task force to move in at any time to take Kodiak and the mainland of Alaska, and we constantly patrolled this area in severe weather conditions.

Lt. Col. Jack Chennault, 343 Group Commanding Officer at Umnak, Alaska in the Aleutians.

As we moved down the chain from Elmendorf to Naknek, then Cold Bay, and finally, Umnak, we were on patrol from dawn to dusk. When we went up, we had to be ready to return to the field fast for a landing as the storm weather fronts swept across the island. There was no radar system to guide us, just a small map with a compass superimposed on it so that we knew what heading to take to get back to the field or which heading to take to search for a suspected Japanese plane coming into our area.

In February our commanding officer joined us at Umnak just before we moved down to the big base at Adak. He was Lt. Col. Jack Chennault, the son of General Chennault of Flying Tiger fame in China. Our C.O. had his own flying Tiger painted on the cowl of our P-40 Tomahawks. General Chennault had a Tiger Shark emblazoned on his plane, and it must have been the press that called them the Flying Tigers. In any event, we didn't mind letting a little of their glory rub off on our group.

Weather conditions were so severe during those months that some of our flights lasted only minutes. My notes show that on one mission we were called to return to the base as fast as possible and even though the flight lasted only five minutes, I couldn't even see the tower at the far end of the runway when I touched down on the ground. We not only had the weather fronts moving in fast but also fierce winds that blew in all directions at once and were a constant hazard. These winds were called "williwaws," and they were something to be wary of.

The Flying Tiger P-40 ground looped.

Much later we learned that the winter of 1942/43 was the worst weather in the last thirty-four years. This was certainly not what we had anticipated.

The bombers shot down over Kiska and Attu were a small number lost compared to the losses from this severe weather condition.

A large Japanese naval force was reported moving into the area at this time, and the rumor was that they were attempting to resupply the island of Kiska. We were all on alert, and the weather conditions made it imperative that we fly constant patrols. We had to be on the flight line with the first light in the sky.

This was not too difficult during the winter months because the days were very short, but as spring approached and the days lengthened, we had to be on flight line at 4 a.m. and remain there until 10 p.m.

We not only flew constant patrols, weather permitting, but we also practiced emergency scrambles. Our crew chiefs kept our planes warmed up during the day because when the scramble call came, we dashed out, started the engines and buckled up, all at the same time. We taxied into position and took off two at a time – accomplishing these emergency take-offs in as little as five minutes.

However, vicious storms blowing through the islands sometimes kept us grounded for days at a

In front of the Flying Tiger flanked by Lts. Dan McFarland Park and Joe R. Foote. Umnak, January 1943.

This sheep skin coat and boots, fur mittens and blanket-lined pants helped keep me warm in minus 55 degree howling winds.

time, and it took us an hour and a half to make what should have been a ten-minute ride to the mess hall during some of these storms.

Our housing was in quonset huts, and the snow often was piled higher than the roofs. We had to keep paths cleared down to the doors.

Our cots and double sleeping bags kept us warm during the night even though a layer of snow had dusted our sleeping bags by morning. The storms blew the snow right through the joints of the hut. When nature called during the night, it was miserable to climb out of the sleeping bag, go outside, climb to the top of the snow bank and test the direction of the blizzard before relieving oneself. And since the wind came from all directions, it wasn't much help to check the wind.

At Adak the snow covered our quonset hut living quarters.

From Adak, the P-38s, B-24s, B-17s, B-26s, and B-25s were able to bomb the Japanese and the P-40s, with their shorter range, patrolled around our island base. The B-24s also were making reconnaissance flights out to the west to keep track of the Japanese fleet. A very small airstrip was carved out of the tundra at Amchitka and some of our P-40s were now within range of Kiska only 40 miles away. On March 24 I flew to Amchitka in a C-47, where there was a very short landing strip. On the north end was a small revetment with the water on the other side. The south end faced a hill with a shallow gully curving off to the right at the very end of the runway. Takeoffs could be made into the wind in either direction, but all landings had to be made from the water no matter which way the wind was blowing. The living conditions on Adak were nothing to brag about but they were luxurious compared to what we found on this forward post.

Unknown to us our navy was searching deep into the North Pacific for the Japanese fleet. In the early morning hours of March

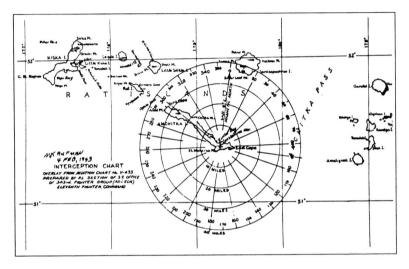

An interception chart strapped to my knee was the only thing we fighter pilots had in one of the worst weather spots in the world.

26 the Naval Battle of Komandorskis (100 miles south of the Russian Komandorski Islands) was taking place. Little did we realize that the fate of the Aleutian Islands would be sealed within the hour.

The American fleet led by Admiral McMorris was composed of one heavy and one light cruiser with four destroyers. They were searching for what turned out to be Admiral Hosogaya, leading nine fast warships, including four heavy cruisers, protecting three Japanese supply ships heading east for Kiska and Attu. The Americans were out numbered in ships, guns, and size by two-to-one.

As this one-sided battle developed, Admiral McMorris was

concerned about their location in the Pacific. Four hundred miles to the west was the Japanese Gibraltar in their Kurile Islands, within range of the Japanese bombers. It was five hundred miles to our closest U. S. Air Base at Adak, where my squadron was now patrolling for Japanese attacks in our P-40 Warhawks.

In a headlong battle that lasted three and one-half hours, with the American ships with their backs to the "wall," Admiral Hosogaya made a serious mistake. His radio operator mistakenly heard that our bomber strike from Adak was on the way. Also the type of bombs fired from our ships lead him to believe that these were dropped from our B-24 bombers. With this miscalculation of what was happening, he withdrew his forces from the battle.

No serious damage was done to either side but the fate of the Aleutians had been decided. We had no way of knowing that the withdrawal of the Japanese fleet would be their last effort in the North Pacific. A very small force of U. S. Naval ships had accomplished the impossible.

For us on Adak the threat of the Japanese invasion was still real. The battle for the islands of Kiska and Attu were still ahead of us.

April 2, from my diary one week after that battle, "The Japanese convoy was reported to be 200 miles (which was really 400 miles) out, but the transports failed to make it to Kiska."

We were right there in the middle of the theater of operations and we did not know what was going on.

The historians revealed this many decades after the war.

For our forces at that time, the Japanese were still the threat to the United States with their overwhelming naval force in the North Pacific, capable of attacking again to take Dutch Harbor, Kodiak, Anchorage, and establish a beachhead in Alaska.

April 5 was my first combat mission from Amchitka. It was a clear day and the moment I had been waiting for since January 1942, when I became a cadet in Little Rock, Ark. We were carrying

A hazardous short 2000 ft. runway on Amtchitka. A bulkhead
on the landing end a curved hill to navigate on takeoff.

With me were Lts. Paul E. Farber, William Morris Roney,
Charles Felk, George T. Byrne, Grund, and Spigler. We were
leaving on our first combat mission out of Amchitka against Kiska.

a 500-pound bomb and had our target area to go for from the reconnaissance photographs we had studied before take-off. As we approached Kiska, a barren tundra-covered island like the rest of them, we could see the build-up of buildings and defense positions. It looked very peaceful, but as we came over the installations, all hell broke loose and the flak was thick all around us. I found it fascinating seeing these black puffs all around me on this first mission. We dove on our assigned target, strafing all the way down, dropped our bombs, and headed home.

A PBY sea plane normally was assigned to escort us to Kiska, but there was none with us on this mission. The escort would have picked us up out of the water if we had been shot down, but without such help, we had orders, if hit, to get as far from the island as possible. We were told to "belly in" or to bail out but not to be captured on Kiska.

We also were told that we could survive only five to ten minutes in those freezing waters. However, we all returned to the base without problems.

Snow storms and gale winds moved in for a few days, but the Japanese convoy alert was called on April 10 and the first mission was to bomb and strafe targets on Kiska, where fires were left burning, and a second mission was a repeat of the first. The third mission was to bomb and strafe Little Kiska, a small island nearby with more enemy installations. We had no casualties on these missions, but we had been losing pilots to weather and flying conditions ever since my arrival on the chain in January, and that day we lost another pilot on Adak. The men were crashing on take-off, spinning into the ocean or diving straight into the water. It seemed such a shame to lose so many men and to realize we had more to fear from the weather than the Japanese.

Unknown to us, a top secret invasion of Attu was preparing to leave in mid-April from San Francisco. Men had received short sleeve shirts and even warned about the dangers of tropical diseases, all to conceal their destination.

Another tactic was increasing the pressure on Kiska and letting up on the bombing of Attu. For the next twenty-one days, from April 5 to April 25, I had flown 24 combat missions over Kiska, and 13 patrol missions over Amchitka.

On Amchitka this was the closest field to the Japanese held Kiska Island. This is what happened when the runway was too short. We had to navigate up the hill with a sharp turn to the right for takeoff.

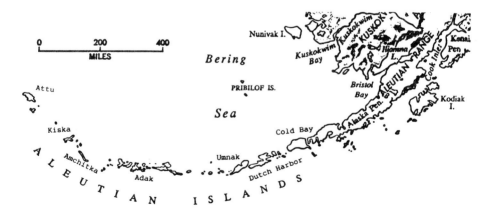

# 5

## Kiska and the Japanese

During April, we continued our missions, sometimes getting lucky as far as the weather was concerned.

My log summed it up:

April 12 – Two missions to bomb Kiska and strafe Little Kiska. Very heavy anti-aircraft fire on the first mission. One of our planes was hit but managed to return to base.

April 14 – We again returned to Kiska to bomb and strafe the runway and the parked sea planes near the beach. The Japanese threw up a wall of anti-aircraft and small-arms fire, but we were very lucky that their accuracy left something to be desired.

April 15 – Three missions today, with fires set in the North Head and Little Kiska area, but we continued to concentrate on the main area of Kiska. Small-arms fire hit my propeller on one of these missions and a B-24 was shot down in flames.

April 16 – Two more missions to the Holtz Bay area and the gun positions on the North Head. This was a very unusual streak of good weather and we were throwing everything we had at the Japanese while we could. Missions flown today against this small island totaled 13 B-24s, 12 B-25s, 32 P-40s, 29 P-38s, and two P-5As.

April 18 – Flew three missions concentrating on the gun placements on the North Head near the submarine base. Since the convoy was unable to get through, they were depending on the submarines to bring in their supplies. When I returned from the last mission, my crew took me over to see a hole in my plane just below the pilot's seat. We searched the cockpit and found a 13.9-MM slug right under where my left leg had been. We had flown through some very intense anti-aircraft and small-arms fire, but I hadn't realized I had been hit until the crew found the hole.

April 19 – Two missions today and for the main target we went after the submarine base and four grounded ships. One of the grounded ships was believed to serve as a power station. It was in flames by the end of the day.

On some of these missions, when we were returning from Kiska, we ran into bad weather and flew by compass heading back toward Amchitka, flying a few feet off the water between the Islands. The moment we saw a faint outline off the island ahead, we would veer left to hug the coastline and head easterly to the field at the far end. The ceiling was so low at times that we would swing around on the water and drop straight in to the field over the dike.

April 20 – Only one mission to Kiska to hit and strafe the ships in the harbor. They were going to find it hard to supply this garrison after the beating we had given them.

Another bad weather front moved in for a few days and it gave us time for much needed rest. The last few days had been a very exhausting period. It was lucky for me, though, that I was such a fatalist. I didn't really believe that any of those shells or bullets were meant for me. My number was not coming up soon, I thought, because I still had too much to do.

April 24 – We lost another pilot. Gorman's plane spun in up at Adak, and we never learned what had caused this crash.

April 25 – Two missions to Kiska bombing and strafing the runway, shipping and submarine base. The second flight was my last mission, and I was then rotated back to Adak to resume patrol duty. I returned in time for the crash of a pilot, Lt. Smith, who went into a hill. His plane was demolished, but he got out with his life. This was his second accident in five days. At the time,

I believed that the crashes and in some case the loss of life, were due to new pilots right out of flying school who had to fly under some of the worst conditions in the world.

I did not believe it possible to regret leaving Amchitka to return to Adak, for this had been a very exciting time in my life, the most exciting period I had ever experienced. I was exhausted after flying 24 missions in 26 days, but I was ready to go on to the next challenge.

In front of the washstand a wall of pin-up photos reminded us what we were fighting for.

The days were getting longer, and we got up at 4 a.m. to trek through the mud of the tundra to get to the mess hall for a breakfast of powdered eggs. After slogging through the mud and cold for several mornings, I decided it wasn't worth the effort and aggravation for such a lousy breakfast. I began sleeping in later – a lesson I remembered the rest of my life. Breakfast wasn't that important, and to this day, I seldom eat breakfast.

We were now back to the routine of patrols, but because of the long days – from 5 a.m. to 10 p.m. – we were on 24 hours and off 24 hours. There were constant scrambles for unidentified aircraft and submarines, but all proved to be false alarms. However, we took nothing for granted, having learned our lesson at Pearl Harbor. We went to any extreme necessary to insure that there would be no surprises in this part of the world.

I very often went up in highly questionable weather to see what it was like away from the field to determine if it was possible to fly patrol. Sometimes I barely made it back before the whole field closed in. We lost two Venturas, most likely caught in the bad weather.

It was May 10 and many new replacements were arriving, but they would have to be broken in before the rest of us could go home. With many new men arriving, I was promoted to flight leader, with a promotion to first lieutenant to follow shortly.

The weather conditions were very bad during this period, and we were still losing planes because of the cold weather. Two P-40s were lost in one day, both on take-off. One pilot made a crash landing two minutes after take-off. Luckily, both pilots climbed out alive. The new pilots were finding it difficult to develop enough respect for the treacherous weather conditions, but one good scare and they began to shape up pretty fast. Those men thought the big danger in the Aleutians would be combat with the Japanese, but they were learning that the big enemies were the williwaws, the sudden, violent, cold winds blowing down from the mountain passes toward the far northern Alaskan coast and the Aleutians.

In mid-May the invasion of Attu was on. The weather was so bad that the bombers and P-38s were unable to give the ground support that was needed. The P-40s were now on patrol starting at 4:00 a.m. every day. Mitsubishi-97 bombers were flying in from Japan to sink our ships at Attu, and P-40s had to remain on alert at Adak at 3:45 a.m. until the Attu invasion was complete. Two P-38s were shot down in the battle at Attu, but we claimed 16 Japanese M-97s.

Our C. O., Lt. Col. James R. Watt, was lost in the Attu invasion on May 24. His last message was: "Followed four Jap bombers vector 270 degrees for 25 minutes. Hit bad, am turning back." He was never heard from again.

I was flying a Canadian P40. Photo taken by a Navy
pilot flying a Kingfisher.

The volcano on Little Sitkin Island. From my P39 I could
fly down close to the erupting volcano. The smoke and
fumes made me keep my distance.

Training the new men in formation, keeping up patrol duty in the air every morning by 4:45 a.m. until 10:50 p.m., and flying with 600 to 1,000-foot ceilings was taking its toll on the men, but by the first week in June, Attu was secured and an airstrip was thrown in to take a squadron of planes.

This had been a very costly invasion for the American forces. We had suffered over 3800 casualties, of which 549 were killed. The Japanese lost over 2400 due to combat and large numbers that committed suicide in the Japanese tradition.

My crew chief Sgt. Vevavdoski servicing my P40 on Adak in the Aleutians. He had to keep our engines warmed up for a scramble takeoff from morning 'til night.

Kiska was still in the hands of the Japanese; so the battle of the Aleutians was not over. Seven P-38s were returning from Kiska on June 11 when the weather closed in at Amchitka, Adak, and Attu and, as they ran out of gas, one went down at Tonopa, two at Adak, three at Atka and one, Lt. Martin, went into the bay. Friedman was saved at Tanaga. The weather was still claiming its toll and was changing from 500 to 1,000-foot ceilings to ground fogs that rolled in and out in a matter of minutes. This was the weather that claimed the P-38s just a few days earlier. Lt. Martin's body was found in the bay a few days after his crash.

We had now received VHF radios to help us cope with these weather conditions. One pilot, Felk, made his first landing in a P-38 with the aid of VHF and was still white as a sheet an hour after landing.

June 21 – The longest day of the year and we were now up at 3:45 a.m. and to bed at 10:30 p.m. I certainly wasn't wasting my time getting up earlier to have powdered eggs in the morning.

Lt. Chapman and bad weather, but a happy ending for him.
He survived.

I asked Lt. George Byrne, a P-38 pilot, to check me out in his plane. I climbed into the cockpit – it was tremendous, the largest plane I had ever seen. He gave me a quick going over, including take-off and landing speeds, starting routine, throttle settings, etc. After a half-hour of studying the instruments, I was ready to fly. I took one flight that day, getting the feel of the plane. There was no doubt that this was a beautiful flying ship. It handled like a million dollars.

The next day I took it up on a much longer flight and this time I did some good acrobatics. But after I landed, I had to admit that even though the P-38 was wonderful, I still preferred my small, single-engine P-40.

June 24 – Orders came through to go home on the first available transportation out. I took the P-40 out for one last flight in very marginal weather and had to return to the field as the weather rolled in. As I landed into the wind, I realized there was a strong wind from the left, then a tail wind, and with much difficulty, I managed to avoid ground-looping. I had been caught in a typical williwaw. I pulled into the parking spot for my plane, cut the engine, and took out my handkerchief and wiped the perspiration off my brow. That was a close call – not dangerous but not the kind of thing to do on the last flight before going home.

Checking out in the P-38. A wonderful twin engine
fighter plane, but still my second choice.

It was at this moment I saw a P-40 coming in for a landing and ground-loop halfway down the runway. Before I could get out to this plane, three other P-40s in the flight came in and all ground-looped on landing. I ran out to the leader's plane, climbed on the wing and saw that it was Captain Bacon, who was also on his last flight before going home. He was not very happy about the situation, but the williwaw had taken its toll of four planes in this one flight.

(Almost two years later, I was flying P-47s at Ibsley in the south of England, when a group of P-47s flew in to our field to stay for a short spell while their own field was being repaired. One of the planes ground-looped on landing, and I jumped on my bicycle and peddled out to commiserate with the unlucky pilot. Imagine my surprise when I climbed onto the wing and greeted Major Bacon.)

A group of us moved up to Elmendorf Field to wait for replacements from the States before we could return home. Flying out of Elmendorf now seemed very easy compared to the islands, but we still lost a lot of planes.

Joe Levy was killed over Kiska, and I believe he was the first P-40 pilot in our outfit to be lost in combat over Kiska as compared to the men we lost because of the weather and flying conditions. A few days later, another pilot, Bradley was shot down over Kiska, but that time a PBY rescue boat was there to pick him up.

Meanwhile, my best friend, Lt. Paul E. Farber, and I had received the Distinguished Flying Cross award. We had been together since cadet training and had flown together from the Island of Amchitka against the Japanese on Kiska. The award was for "missions against the Japanese from advance bases against strong enemy positions. Many missions were over long distances over open water under unfavorable weather conditions. On many of these missions, enemy gun positions were strafed from low altitude."

Finally on August 2, we boarded a plane and flew to Seattle.

Out on the desolate Aleutians Islands, we had not been aware that we were causing such hardship to the native Aleuts, relatives of the Eskimos. The 881 natives had been evacuated "for their own protection" and moved to relocation camps on the mainland. There, they were held in isolation in ramshackle camps and an abandoned fish cannery. They lived in single-walled buildings with rotted floors and smashed windows, and with no toilet facilities and meager supplies. Little did we dream that these gentle people of our own country would have given anything to be treated half as well as we were treating our prisoners of war in the United States.

It took the American people 48 years to make some amends for the miserable two years that the Aleuts lived in these squalid camps.

# 6

## A New Group and the P-47

From Mitchell Field, I went to Westover Field in Massachusetts, and it was here I checked out the P-47 Thunderbolt for the first time. This was like nothing I had ever been in before. It was tremendous. It was powerful, and it was the greatest plane I would ever hope to fly.

I fell in love with it immediately. But I was here only for four days flying transition, formation, and some acrobatics. We then were moved to Hillsgrove Airport in Providence, Rhode Island.

From September 8, 1943 until October 24, we flew intensive training. We practiced flying formation, interceptions, acrobatics, navigation, acrobatics above 20,000 feet, and night flying. It was really hard flying one to three missions a day.

At one point I decided to see how high I could take this plane up. When I got to 35,000 feet, the plane began to get very "mushy." It was really tough, but I pushed it forward and finally at 37,500 feet, it mushed over and began to fall into a spin. I had no problem getting it out of the spin, but I had accomplished what I needed to know – just how much this plane could do.

The weather wasn't too good at this time of the year. Many times we were flying at 1,500 feet, and the ceiling was so low I had trouble locating where I was. All this was good training for combat. Another experience, which for me was new, was flying low level over highly populated areas. One day, flying really low,

I couldn't see a half-mile ahead. Then the next day I was up at 35,000 feet and flying between Boston and New York. I tilted the wing to the left, and I looked down and there was New York, and then I tilted to the right and there was Boston. It was almost as if they were right next to each other.

The next transfer was to William Northern Field in Tullahoma, Tenn. It was here that I joined the 48th Fighter Bomber Group.

On December 12 I received permission to take my plane and fly to my home town, Little Rock, Ark. I called my relatives and told them to meet me at the airport. At this time, we were flying P-47s, P-39s, and P-40s. and so I took a P-40 and flew to Little Rock. Apparently, the civilian airport was not accustomed to seeing military planes land, and so when I landed and jumped out of my plane in my flyer's uniform, I felt like a returning war hero. Everyone treated me like one, and it was a lot of fun to be with my family and friends that day. By nightfall, I was back with my buddies in Tullahoma.

Off and on, I had been able to do skeet shooting as part of the training. This was not only fun, but it also trained fighter pilots in marksmanship at a moving target. The latest thing then was to qualify with a .45-caliber sub-machine gun. I was just hoping they would never have to take me out of my P-47, close to the front lines, to defend the air strip from enemy forces.

But I did qualify expert.

On one mission while still in the states, a group of us had been sent on a training exercise out of Punta Gorda, Fla. We were participating in troop landing exercises off the Gulf Coast. The troops were coming in on the beaches in LST landing craft to practice for the invasion of Normandy in the long-distant future. We received an emergency order to scramble and search the water in the landing area, where we were told there had been an accident. We were told that the wave action at the time of the approach to shore had not been as expected and the boats had dropped their ramps prematurely. With that action, the boats were swamped and men had been lost. Our mission was to look for soldiers in the water. We never found any and never heard any more about the accident, but it showed me again that it didn't take enemy gunfire to lose lives. For the soldier, sailor, and airman, the battle to survive started in training.

In January 1944, the 48th moved to Walterboro, S.C. Some of us had already been in combat in the Pacific, Africa, or Europe, and the commanding officer, Col. Dixon Allison, called us together and told us that the unit was now training to go over to England in the near future.

We knew what that meant – the invasion of Hitler's Europe. We were given the choice of staying with the group or transferring and taking our chance on whatever the future had in store for us. Without any hesitation I chose to stay and go over for the big invasion of Europe. I had no desire to go back to fighting

The beginning of the 48th Fighter Group flying P47s at Punta Gordon. Lts. Joseph S. McMinn, Robert D. Fuller, Edward J. Zienka, Olav Husted, Robert C. Young, and Fredrick J. Larner. Squadron C.O. Capt. Richard P. Morrissey and Lts. John J. Adam, Jr., and John E. Benbow who ended up in Stalag Luft I with me.

the Japanese again, and the European Theater was pulling at me. As a Jew, I especially felt called to fight against Hitler and his Nazis.

However, my best friend, Paul Farber, made a different choice. He had been with me since Hamilton Field in 1942, flying our first fighter planes and then in combat against the Japanese in the Aleutians. He chose to stay behind and ended up in the China-Burma Theater flying P-47s.

At Walterboro, I had a chance to practice serial gunnery for the first time. Most of the pilots were new, and I quickly realized the value of experience. The new pilots made few hits on the cloth sleeves towed by the target planes, while the men coming from the African, Aleutian, and European theaters had no trouble filling the sleeves with holes. The bullets we used were color-coded with wet paint so that when the mission was over and the cloth sleeves were dropped, the color marks left on the sleeve could be credited easily to the right pilot in the missions.

All the month of February this group settled down for some intense training in aerial bombing and gunnery, all this in preparation to go to England. During that month, I flew 18 aerial gunnery and bombing missions plus some instrument and night flying practice.

Finally, by March 1, I had my last flight in the U. S, and began moving out – first to Camp Shanks, New York, a holding camp, and then to New York for Scotland. We sailed on the "Queen of the Seas" – the Queen Mary – a beautiful ship with part of her glory still visible.

Since I was a first lieutenant, I had a "small" stateroom – which I shared with 27 other men. The hammocks were four deep, floor to ceiling, and not all of us could stand on the floor at the same time. The hammocks were so close together that to turn over, I had to get out of the bunk and get back in. But we each had a bunk of our own. When I went to the lower areas of the ship where the troops were housed, compared to conditions there, I realized we were living in the lap of luxury. Their hammocks were just as close together, but huge numbers of men were crammed into rooms which had no proper ventilation. A large number of these men shared their hammocks with other soldiers so that the decks were full of men at all times, taking turns sleeping. We were told there were 17,000 men on board.

Our ship sailed alone from New York. We depended only on our speed to outrun any Germans in the Atlantic. The captain changed course every 10 minutes or so, and I was told had new orders that he opened every day to get his course headings. Rumors were always running rife of German wolfpacks moving in on us.

In our group there was a non-flying officer who was supposed to have flown to England to prepare our base for our arrival. It turned out he was afraid to make the flight in a bomber and he turned up on the ship with us. Even though there were strict regulations against starting unfounded rumors, we couldn't resist setting this man up. When we told him that the ship's captain had confirmed that we were being stalked by a large German submarine wolfpack ahead of us, he was so frightened that we finally told him the truth.

The crossing took five days, and after landing in Glasgow, Scotland, we entrained immediately for southern England, arriving at our new home at a small hamlet called Ibsley near the village of Ringwood, Hampshire. This was a beautiful, serene part of the English countryside.

VULNERATUS·NON·VICTUS

## *Chain of Command 48th Fighter Bomber Group*

|  |  |
|---|---|
| Group Commander | Col. George C. Wertenbaker |
| Deputy Group Commander | Lt. Col. James A. Dowling |

### *494th Squadron*

|  |  |
|---|---|
| Squadron Commander | Capt. Richard P. Morrissey |
| Operation Officer | Capt. Charles R. Fischette |

### *Flight Commanders*

|  |  |
|---|---|
| Flight A | Capt. John W. Watson |
| Flight B | First Lt. Victor Cabas |
| Flight C | Capt. Moss K. Fletcher |
| Flight D | First Lt. Mozart Kaufman |

The rank of these officers changed often because they were promoted very quickly after we went into combat in April 1944.

The number of pilots in a squadron varied from month to month depending on replacements, loss of pilots in combat, transfers, and leaves.

In combat, the full complement on a mission was:

|  |  |
|---|---|
| Flight | Four planes |
| Squadron | 16 planes |
| Group | 48 planes |

# 7

## Combat over Europe

Ibsley Field was set in the middle of beautiful rolling farmland in southern England. Our quarters were rows of small buildings with individual rooms, one for each officer. Soon after arriving we were issued bicycles, which turned out to be the best presents we could have received. Not only could we use the bikes to get to our planes, but also they gave us the ability to be independent in wartime England and to roam the countryside when we had leave.

It was a wonderful sight to see our P-47s parked all over the field waiting for us to take over. I had flown my last flight March 1 at Walterboro Air Field, South Carolina, in a P-39. Now, on April 8, I was taking off on my first test flight in England in a P-47. It was an exhilarating feeling but even more so because of the lovely surroundings. From the train coming down from Scotland it had been beautiful to see, but from the air, it was another dimension. The small villages and farms were unlike anything I had seen in the United States. Here I was seeing a civilization that had developed over hundreds of years.

The first week we flew one or two flights a day, practicing formation, mock combat, and ground gunnery, familiarizing ourselves with the area. On April 16 Capt. Richard Morrissey, our commanding officer, led his flight leaders and the pilots who had flown previously in combat to Chilbolton, a field just 30 miles away, to join another squadron of experienced pilots who had been flying combat missions out of England for some time. On April 18 we flew a formation warm-up in the morning and in the afternoon, we set out on our first mission across the English Channel. This mission was to escort B-26s on a bombing attack of Charleroi, Belgium, and back. The next day we escorted 250 B-17s to an area near Liege, Belgium,

Standing on the wing of my P47 in France. This was an old model canopy before the new bubble canopies came out.

and home. Both of these missions were three-hour flights, and we had to climb through thick overcast skies to stay with the bombers. However, they were uneventful "milk runs," and not the excitement I had been anticipating. After another mission on April 19 was called off, our indoctrination with this group was finished. With the number of combat missions we had flown on prior tours of duty, we needed no more of this practice.

The next day we returned to Ibsley, where we had intense training for the next week in dive-bombing, group formations, and camera aerial gunnery, flying up to as many as four flights a day. We, obviously, were preparing for a full schedule of bomber escort missions and fighter bombing missions.

We knew the invasion of the Continent was coming and that the reason we were called the 48th Fighter Bomber Group was that we would be bombing and strafing in support of ground troops when the time came.

One of the types of training we received involved being assigned an area of the countryside in which to practice flying at ground level. I led my flight of four, flying as low as possible – the ultimate dream of every pilot. I swept over the countryside at 250 miles an hour and, as I came to a small cottage, I would raise my wing slightly to keep from hitting it and then level off back to five to ten feet above the ground. Even though I raised my wings to avoid bushes and shrubs, it was not surprising to land and find bits of greenery clinging to the wings.

I hoped that the English people had been evacuated from their homes in this training area, as our low flying would seem to have created chaos in cottages filled with china and knickknacks.

Finally, on May 1, we went on our first mission to France, a fighter sweep to St. Maurice-Mortain. Although we ran into light flack, it seemed another milk run. However, we were tired from a very intense period of flying that for me had meant 29 flights since April 8, and I was looking forward to a short period of rest and perhaps using my bicycle to explore the English countryside. Until now, I had only been able to ride the bike to and from my plane.

The town of Ibsley, where we were stationed, was a charming village with rows of small cottages. We found that the English residents lived up to their reputations of loving gardens and neat little houses. My best friend and assistant flight leader, Lt. Johnny Staring, and I rode our bikes to the nearby village of Ringwood, which also was a delightful town with cobblestone streets and stone bridges like on a postcard. From there we went north to an old Saxon village called Fordingbridge. I had always been attracted to small towns and villages and I could not get enough of exploring the ones nearby.

On the first weekend I had a leave, I took a bus to Salisbury, where I saw the magnificent Gothic cathedral that is one of the most famous in England. The beauty of this cathedral and its grounds were absolutely unsurpassed by anything I had seen in America. I was not aware then that the cathedral was also well known because of the paintings of it in the 19th century by John Constable, one of England's greatest artists. Little did I realize that some day I would learn to paint and would study Constable's paintings as the epitome and style of what I wanted to accomplish.

The inside of the cathedral was overwhelming, but the most impressive thing to me was the age of the structure. In some areas of the church prominent people had been buried under the slabs of the floor more than 200 years before Columbus discovered America. To this Southern boy from Vicksburg, "ancient" meant as far back as the American Civil War.

But after a few days of sightseeing and visiting local pubs, it was time to get back to work again.

According to the record, on May 4 I was promoted to captain. I mention this because promotion orders were written high up in the chain of command and God only knows when I found out about it.

The next two days we carried out fighter sweeps to Angers, Nantes, Chateau-Dun, and Paris. On the missions to Paris the Germans had plenty of anti-aircraft guns waiting for us. We encountered the most intense flak we had run into not only over Paris but also all the way to the coast of France. I had flown through heavy flak in the Aleutians, but this was much more than the Japanese had used against us.

As we made our way back over the channel after one of the missions, we spotted a British pilot in the water off the coast of France. We radioed back to England with the location of the downed pilot, but we could not stay long enough to rescue him. We never did learn if he was picked up by the British or whether the Germans got to him first. When we landed, we discovered flak and small-arms fire holes all over our own planes.

Then came two more days of escorting B-26s to Namur and A-20s to Bourquenaison. Over this target on the second day, there was a great deal of flak. I was flying side by side with one of the B-20s, which was no more than three plane lengths away, when it was hit by a burst of flak. I watched the bomber blow up and actually disappear from the sky. There was nothing left but charred pieces floating around.

The next two days, May 10 and 11, saw the beginning of the work we had been trained to do, with three missions of concentrated dive bombing of the marshalling yards at Rouen, France, and the next day at Tourcoing. We had seen six freight trains of 10 cars each, and diving from 12,000 feet we released our bombs at 6,000 feet. We did a thorough bombing not only on the trains but also the roundhouse and repair shops, leaving them in a smoking mess.

The next mission to Valenciennes was a repeat of the previous mission, diving from 13,000 feet and releasing our bombs at 3,500 feet, leaving a roundhouse and train sheds in flames and smoke. On these last missions we had run into heavy flak, but only one pilot, Lt. Richard Williams, suffered heavy damage but he managed to make it home despite holes in his wings. One look at his plane convinced the rest of us that we could not be too smug or too careful.

(Thirty years later when I visited Rouen, I was grateful that our targets in 1944 were outside of this beautiful city and that we were able to leave historical buildings intact.)

In the middle of May, after 10 missions in 11 days, I had two days off and decided to take a bus to Bournemouth in the county of Dorset, a famous seaside resort. Walking along the beach and watching English children collecting shells and building sand castles was just what I needed – a complete change of scenery from bombing and destruction. However, a week later after a vacation and one milk-run escort to Rennes, I was itching for action.

# 8

## The Lull before the Storm

On May 20 we took off early in the morning for a dive-bombing mission to Cambrai. We ran into overcast weather on the way there, but over the target, there was a different story. The Germans were waiting for us with heavy flak, and although the mission was successful, one of our pilots, Capt. Thompson Litchfield, was hit and reported to have bailed out about 15 miles inland. Another pilot also was shot down and they both ended up as prisoners of war.

Early each morning we received briefings about the kind of missions for which we had been waiting. No more milk runs – now we were flying down on the deck, bombing marshalling yards, bridges and moving targets, hitting them with machine gun fire and our bombs. Needless to say, this kind of fighting brought more casualties, but this kind of action was what we had asked for.

There was a morning mission to Rennes, Brittany, but we had to turn back because of overcast weather. Then when it cleared by afternoon, we set forth again to knock out any rolling stock we found. My enjoyment of viewing the French countryside from above was broken by the sight of a train rolling along carrying supplies. I called for my flight to follow me, telling them I would take the train's engine and they were to take the box cars. The white smoke that erupted after our hits somehow added to the illusion of beauty of the quiet country scene, and for the moment "war" was forgotten.

We made more attacks on trains in this area and ended up with three locomotives to our credit that time. Then it was time to head north and back to England. As I approached the coast, I spotted a strange sight looming out of the sea. There was a huge rock surrounded by water with ancient buildings layered one on top of another and topped by a church and steeple. I wanted to circle around to see it more clearly, but that didn't seem the time to play games. We had to head home before it got dark, and it wasn't until I got back to England that I realized I had seen one of the the great wonders of France, Mont-St-Michel. (Thirty-five years later I visited this glorious structure and recalled my first glimpse.)

On that flight in 1944, after checking my map, Mont-St-Michel gave me the clue I needed to lead my flight on the right compass heading to England and Ibsley. Half-way back we began to run into heavy weather and I decided to climb over the top of it. I had been on the radio with my flight, but I switched to the channel where I could get weather information about southern England. There was a solid overcast, even on the east side of England, where bombers and fighters were returning from Germany, Belgium, and France. Everyone was screaming for help, trying to determine locations and gain directions for landing.

There was no way we could make contact through that mess, and so I switched back to my men and informed them that we were on our own. We didn't have the slightest idea how low the ceiling was or if there was any ceiling at all. I figured that we were very close to the English coastline and then all at once, I spotted a cluster of flak that had been shot at our planes. This was a clue that we were over England and that our planes were being mistaken for enemy aircraft. I had a feeling we might have been over the coastal town of Portsmouth, and so we turned east where our base should be. A few minutes later, I saw a tiny break in the clouds and there below was the lovely green English terrain. I alerted my flight and said, "Here we go. Follow me." I took a wing over and my three men followed me right through the hole, finding a ceiling of a good 2,000 feet below us, plenty of room in which to fly home. This had been a very successful group mission with 11 locomotives attacked, four of them seen to explode, and numerous box cars strafed.

The next day there was another major group bombing mission led by a Major McCabe and headed towards Antwerp. There were 53 P-47s, each of us armed with two 1,000-pound bombs. But 13 of the planes were lost climbing through clouds in bad weather and had to return to England. When we arrived at the target at Aerschot, only eight aircraft dropped their bombs on the marshalling yard. We continued on to the secondary target at Hamme. I was on this bomb run and made six good hits on a marshalling yard where we ran into very heavy flak. This mission had been dispatched at 6:24 p.m. and we did not return until 10:20 p.m.

Early the next day at 6:18 a.m., Major Morrissey, our squadron commander who had just been promoted, was dispatched to lead 51 P-47s on an escort of B-24s. This was a very unusual order because it called for a start-up of engines at 6:56 a.m. and take-off just 10 minutes later at 7:06. a.m. There was little time for navigational data and briefing of pilots, and with the rush, the 51 planes took off at 7:12 a.m., six minutes late. Major Morrissey pushed the throttle forward and made up time, and we arrived at our rendezvous with the bombers on schedule.

We met with 400 bombers, and by radio identified some 120 to 180 B-24s we were to escort to the limit of our endurance to the Orleans/Bricy Airfield. The balance of the mission was for us uneventful, light flak and no German planes.

After more than 45 years, I have no memory of what we did for food on these two missions. We had flown a three and a half hour mission the night before and then started off early again the next morning for another mission of three hours and 20 minutes. I guess we must have survived on K rations in between.

On Saturday, May 27, I had a couple of days off and left

for a visit to London, excited because I had never been there. I looked up some relatives of my married sister and visited with them in their quarters at the Grosvenor House, where I had a nice dinner and spent a pleasant evening. The next day I visited all the famous sights I had heard about – the changing of the guard at Buckingham Palace and Piccadilly Circus. I also shopped in the stores, so different from the ones in America, and finished off the day with a performance of the musical, "Panama Hattie" by Cole Porter. I still have the program, for which I was charged 10 pence. As I remember, some food and drinks were sold at the seats, much like at an American baseball game.

Even with the buzz bombs overhead, it was a thrill to be in famous London town. I did feel sorry, though, for the residents who had to live with the threat of bombings every day. All through the day and night I heard the ominous sound of a bomb approaching and then passing over and exploding in the distance. It was a very eerie feeling realizing that those people, not soldiers, but women and children, were living under this threat month after month, stretching into years.

When I returned to the field the next day, I learned that one of our pilots, Lt. Carlos Ball, had died in a tragic take-off accident during an operational flight. His plane was carrying a 1,000-pound bomb, and during an attempt to extinguish the fire and rescue the pilot after the crash, the bomb exploded. Twelve men were injured, and two of them subsequently died.

On the same day, two pilots, Lt. Robert Price and Capt. Robert Fuller, bailed out over France during a bombing mission of a railroad underpass led by our commanding officer, Major Morrissey.

I had scheduled myself to lead my flight the next day, May 29, and in the morning, I heard heavy footsteps pounding down the hall. My door opened, and a loud voice announced, "Five o'clock mission call." I jumped out of my warm bed into a cold room that felt like the Quonset hut in the Aleutians. I took my time getting ready, having learned in the Aleutians to pass up the lousy powdered egg breakfasts and either sleep longer or take my time dressing.

The pilots scheduled for the mission gathered in the ready room for briefing. There was a map of Europe on the wall with lines drawn from our air field to our target in Germany. First, the intelligence officer gave us details of the mission, an escort for a major B-17 bombing mission returning from Leipzig, where they were to bomb aircraft factories and assembly plants. They were to be escorted from England half way to the target by P-47s and then long-range P-51s would take over. We were to meet the bombers half way back and provide cover home. I had my pad attached to a small board, with a map on which I wrote all the information I would need. I had written compass headings, the time to meet the bombers, and a complete run-down on the German defenses we would run into, heavy or light anti-aircraft fire, etc. On the pad, as well as on the back of my hand, I had written the times I would need first, when to start the engine, take off, and rendezvous.

After a weather officer gave us a run-down on what to expect, the commander of the group gave final instructions on the flight. He was leading the full group, three squadrons, for a total of 48 P-47s. We then set our watches to the second, and I strapped the pad to my leg and headed to my plane.

I climbed into the cockpit, and my crew chief stood on the wing and helped buckle me in and gave me a pat on the shoulder and a thumbs-up sign. I did the check list before starting the engine and then I was ready. I checked the time, watched the minute hand and then counted down 20 seconds – 15, 10, 5, 4, 3, 2, 1, 0 – and watched my leader as I started my engine.

One after another, we pulled out of our parking spaces and slowly "ess-ed" toward the take-off point. At the end of the runway, we wasted no time in taking off in pairs. Climbing in a controlled circle, we formed up in formation and headed east for our rendezvous with the bombers over Nazi Germany.

This was my first experience in escorting a large group from a mission of this type. We were in an area about 25 miles southwest of Coblenz, Germany, when I spotted a single plane coming toward us, but as we got closer, I realized it was not one plane but a cluster of them, it looked like a swarm of hornets. As the group approached, I saw that this was the vast armada of B-17s returning from a mission deep into Germany. We escorted them back, learning later that 34 of those heavy bombers from the Eighth Air Force had been shot down over Germany during that one day.

That afternoon we had a dive-bombing mission to France to wipe out an air field at Vannes. We ran into medium flak over the target, but put our bombs right on the nose. During the mission in the morning, we had seen no flak, but the importance of that escort operation had been our most important job for the day.

By now the thing uppermost in our minds was "when will the invasion of Hitler's fortress begin?" We were like prize fighters honed up to the moment of the world's championship match. We were ready and this was why I had chosen almost six months ago to stay with the 48th and go to England

The last two days of May were spent in escorting B-17s to Reims and Belgium, which turned out to be my last successful mission before the invasion.

On June 1 the weather took a turn for the worst. Wind and rain made it impossible for us to fly, and unknown to us, General Eisenhower and his staff were being forced to make decisions beyond what a single person should have to do. The vast armada that had been assembled would have to start moving the night before the date chosen as the ideal morning to launch the invasion. The general had scheduled the invasion for Monday, June 5.

This date was chosen because the moon and the tide were at the maximum depth for landing craft to unload thousands of men and thousands of tons of material on the landing beaches at dawn.

But on the early morning of June 4, the general still could not make the decision to order the vast armada to move. By Sunday night, with high winds shrieking outside and rain lashing at his headquarters, it was obvious his decision was correct. With this weather, there was no chance to predict when the invasion would start. Since boats and ships already had left England for France, planes and patrols were sent out to turn them back. Using the radio was out of the question during a time of complete radio blackout. Some of the boats were turned back almost in sight of France.

But Sunday night, weather forecasters were predicting that the storm would let up and it would be clear for an invasion on Tuesday, June 6. The final decision was reached Monday morning and if General Eisenhower had not taken this gamble, he would have had to wait another two weeks for a favorable tide.

The pilots at Ibsley continued to bombard our targets, but when we attempted to fly to Paris, we had to turn back at Rouen because of weather. The result was that during the highly emotional time between June 1 and June 5, I had done almost nothing. The field had been buttoned up and there were no passes for anyone to leave.

# 9

## The Invasion

When we went to bed Monday, June 5, we were unaware that the invasion had already started. While we slept, ships had left the ports of England, and transport planes full of paratroopers were on their way to Normandy, where they would be dropped inland from the beaches. Their mission would be to hold key bridges, crossroads and other strategic positions.

When the door of my room opened early on the morning of June 6, and a loud voice called out a mission wake-up, I knew this was "it."

In the briefing room, a map of Normandy was spread out on the wall while we received our instructions. The weather had cleared up over Normandy, and we were to climb up through a weather front on the way.

Major Morrissey was leading the squadron of 16 planes, each armed with two 500-pound bombs and a belly gas tank. My Flight D was to be the lead flight, and I was chosen to be Major Morrissey's wing man. The intelligence officer gave us a complete run-down of the mission and showed us photographs of our targets. We were told that all we would see was a large hedgerow and in the corner of this hedgerow, there would be a well camouflaged gun battery, which was our target.

Take-off time was scheduled for 5:35 a.m. and we set our watches to the second. We took off on schedule and as we flew out over the channel, we climbed up to the cloud cover. We knew how important it was that every plane stay in formation and stick together. On prior missions, planes had become lost in the clouds and, unable to find the group, were forced to abort and return to the base.

The 16 planes of my squadron were spread out in a long V formation. As we entered the cloud cover, we closed in, wing tip to wing tip. We all knew that if one pilot got out of line, it would affect the rest of the squadron, much like the effect of cracking a whip. Any irregular movement by the planes closest to the leader would affect the tail-end Charlie the most.

After we had climbed 2,000 to 3,000 feet into the clouds, I saw that Major Morrissey was banking slightly to the right. I thought that he had vertigo and didn't realize that he was going off course. I hung on, and it got worse and worse, and I thought if we didn't straighten out, we would lose the whole squadron. Even though I didn't dare take my eyes off the leader, I took a quick look at the needle that showed the bank and turn to see how far off we were. We were flying absolutely straight ahead, and I was the one with the vertigo. However, just looking at the needle pointing straight up made my vertigo disappear.

At 7,000 feet, we broke through the clouds into sunshine. The entire squadron was in a perfect formation, and a few minutes later, we arrived on schedule at 6:20 a.m., spotting the Normandy coastline below. It was the most dramatic sight I had ever seen. Below was the largest armada every assembled. From the air, it looked like a small boy had dumped a box of wooden matches into his tub of bath water. There were battleships, cruisers, destroyers, and landing craft of all shapes and sizes by the thousands. We could only imagine what the crossfire between the Allies and Germans would be.

Major Morrissey headed right for our target. We recognized the shape of the lot we were looking for and we saw that it was surrounded by hedgerows. We knew that in the corner of the hedgerows was our target, but that we wouldn't be able to see it for the camouflage. We also knew we were going after one of the big guns.

Dick Morrissey spotted the target and motioned for the squadron to follow. As he peeled off, we followed, one after another, diving straight down in an attempt to get near enough to drop our bombs on the small intersection of hedgerows.

We dropped our bombs and got good results on the battery of guns. Our mission was completed, and we headed back over the channel to England. I took my last look at the remarkable armada spread out below me, with the small craft headed for the French coast and the large ships firing their big guns. When we returned to Ibsley at 7:40 a.m., everyone there wanted to know what it had been like.

It was a wonderful experience, being on the first mission of our squadron on the first day of the invasion on June 6, 1944.

I later learned that our target had been one of a cluster of deadly German 170-mm guns. These guns had a range of 18 miles and were so mobile that the Germans seldom fired more than two shells from the same spot while under attack. Our allied intelligence officers had reported eight of them had been knocked out. I hoped that we were responsible for destroying one of them.

After lunch I headed to the ready room to find out about my next assignment. The next mission was posted on the board, and I saw that Flight D, my flight, was scheduled to go on the second mission of the invasion that afternoon. The big surprise was to see my name leading the mission. I had never led a squadron in combat before, and I thought they had made a mistake. I checked with the major, and he said, "It's all yours."

After a briefing and looking at the map showing in detail the location of another coastal gun emplacement, we made a repeat of the morning mission, going back to the area of Grandcamp, right on the beach. There the activity below was even more tremendous than it had been in the morning. I located the target and led the squadron down for a successful bombing run. It was a great feeling to know that we were the arm supporting our troops on the ground.

On June 7 at 7:47 a.m., our group led by the commanding officer, Col. George L. Wertenbaker, took off with 48 P-47s to escort 100 tug and glider combinations of "Mission Hackensack." The gliders stretched half-way across the channel, and we stayed with them for three and a half hours, weaving back and forth from one end to the other between England and France, making sure that no German fighter could get through to them.

It was hard to believe that the gliders, so flimsily made of plywood and loaded with troops, would belly land in the fields. It was especially dangerous because the fields were covered with steel traps laid by German General Rommel's troops in anticipation of just such a move by the Allies. We hovered over the gliders until they appeared to have made safe landings and then we returned to our base in England.

In the afternoon, I led the squadron on another dive bombing mission to the same Grandcamp area. The ships at sea were still shelling the coast, and the Allies had such complete superiority that no German fighter planes had attempted to join the fray.

When I returned from that mission, I heard the sad news that one of our pilots, Lt. Norm Johnson, had been shot down over enemy territory and there was no word of his survival. However, when two more pilots returned, we were told that Norm had been seen crash-landing near Turqueville, getting out of his plane and waving to the other pilots before running to nearby woods.

The next day, June 8, we had a very pleasant surprise when Norm walked into our air base. He told us how he had made his way to the French coast on foot and then found a ride back to England. What a thrill it was to see my pal walking into that base when we thought he was lost.

Three days later, 36 P-47s flew as a group to the beach area, where we divided up into three squadrons of 12 each to patrol our respective areas. Shortly after talking with one of our crew members in England on the radio, we received a call back asking our position. Since the voice was different from the first call, our group leader answered with a challenge. The only reply was, "I do not understand you."

Our leader repeated the challenge, receiving the same reply. We assumed the voice on the radio was that of the enemy. This was my only experience with this sort of thing, but later I read about it happening to other pilots.

Shortly afterward, eight FW-190 German fighters attacked one of our flights and shot down First Lt. Richard Ried. When his plane was hit, his belly tank caught fire and the tail of his plane exploded. He was seen bailing out and descending in his parachute.

However, for the next five days, I flew four patrol missions, still without seeing a single German plane.

By June 10, a remarkable four days after the invasion, American engineers were ready to begin their work of constructing a 5,000-foot air field at the small town of Cordonville on the main highway between Bayeaux and Carenton. This was to be one of three air fields for the P-47s waiting in England to move across the channel. Just four days later they completed construction of our future air strip at Deux-Jumeaux, which would be known as "A-4." Meanwhile, there was fighting going on all around and snipers were still taking shots at the engineers as they worked.

On June 15 I led the squadron on a dive-bombing mission to hit the fuel dumps at Conde-s-Vire, just below St. Lo. We had good hits in that area.

That night I learned that my pal Norm Johnson had been shot down again. The other pilots on his mission reported that he was hit at low altitude behind enemy lines and had crashed with his plane bursting into flames. He had not been seen getting out of the plane. Norm and I had been together for more then two years, starting out at Hamilton Field in California and then

Alaska, the Aleutians, and from one air field to another in the states and, finally in England.

We had stood together in the line when Colonel Allison had posed the question about volunteers for the European theater, and we both had chosen to go to England for the invasion. Norm was a mild, quiet man. When guys around him were using curse words, his only expression was "Oh fluff!" He came from Salt Lake City and perhaps that explained some of why he was that way. I would really miss him.

Two days later we flew top fighter cover for a B-26 escort mission. The Jerrys were around below and were trying to evacuate that area of La Have Dup Coutances. I dove down to attack, but after a few minutes of searching to no avail, I returned as top cover.

On D Day Plus 12, or June 18, our 48th group in Ibsley was planning its own invasion – to move to the new air strip in France. However, for me that day started early in the morning with leading my flight of four on regular missions. The first mission was to Road Vire and then to Ville Dieu. We had two 500-pound bombs and a belly tank of gas. We crossed the channel and located the road we were scheduled to patrol, and I spotted a large truck filled with troops. To save my bombs for larger targets, I dove down and dropped my gas tank right in the open back of the truck and then told my men to strafe and set fire to the truck. There was a huge explosion, and we continued on.

(In 1992, 47 years later, I got a call from Bill Johnson in Santa Cruz Calif. I had not seen him since July 1944. He was then Lt. William Johnson and we had been together in the states. He reminded me that he had been the element lead (two planes) in that flight, and he told me that after I had bombed the truck with my gas tank, his element strafed the truck and he left a fireball in the sky. He said he thought that that was the beginning of napalm bombing.)

Instead of flying back to England, which was normal pro-cedure after an attack, we flew a short distance to A-3, the new landing site at Cordonville. After we were briefed about our next mission, we discovered the place was swarming with reporters looking for stories about any activity surrounding the landing of the first P-47s in France. One of my men mentioned the gas tank incident, and reporters made a big thing of it. The wire services ran stories all over the United States, and an article appeared in my hometown paper in Little Rock, Ark. The good thing was that my family learned I had been promoted to captain.

We took off from Cordonville for our next mission to dive-bomb an ammunition dump at Foret de St. Sever. We hit the target and confirmed a successful mission. We were scheduled for

## Turns Nazi Vehicles Into Flaming Pyres.

CAPT. MOZART KAUFMAN.
An Allied Landing Field in

France, June 18 (Delayed) (AP).— Capt. Mozart Kaufman of 208 Crystal street, Little Rock, Ark., didn't want to waste a bomb on a German van and trailer today, so he skip-bombed his half-empty bellytank of gasoline into the vehicles and then set them ablaze with incendiary bullets.

Captain Kaufman was piloting a P-47 equipped with a bomb under each wing when he spotted the large van and trailer snealing down a side road.

Captain Kaufman, formerly assistant manager of Sterling Stores in North Little Rock, is a nephew of Sam Grundfest, president of Sterling Stores, Inc. He entered the army in October, 1940, was trained at Leavenworth, Kan., and then transferred to the Army Air Forces.

After flight training at California and Texas air fields he was in the Aleutian islands for 18 months. He returned here on a 60-day leave and was sent to England in February, 1944. While here, he lived in the home of Morris Ehrenberg, 208 Crystal street. His mother, Mrs. Ruby Kaufman, lives in New York city.

From my home town paper of Little Rock, Arkansas.

two more missions that afternoon out of A-3, the first to be top-cover escorts for bombers bombing the same area where I had been, and the second to an air field at Lessay, a reconnaissance area for Coutances and Carentan. This was very close support for the troops, and we were clobbering the hell out of the Germans.

Following the fifth mission of the day and debriefing, we headed back to Ibsley, England, where we landed at 9:30 p.m. I remember that the day had been so hectic that either there had been no time for meals or there had been none available yet at the new quarters in France. In any event, all I had eaten all day was one package of K rations. However, when I finally got back to the base after flying five missions, I was too tired to eat and I went straight to bed.

Considering that it was now only D-Day plus 12, the engineers and ground troops had made remarkable accomplishments. On June 18, our 48th Group ground personnel at Ibsley began packing for the move to France. It took two weeks to complete the move to our new base, A-4, in Normandy.

The city of Cherbourg, a port city at the top of the Cherbourg Peninsula, had been deemed of utmost importance for the Allies. If ground troops could take this city, the allies would gain a deep-water port necessary for unloading the millions of tons of material and troops.

On June 22, I led the squadron of 47 P-47s on a mission which was coordinated with P-47s throughout southern England. Orders were to sweep across the area south of the city of Cherbourg and to dive-bomb and strafe the Germans at the front line. We had specific instructions to start the run at 1:15 p.m. and to complete the run at 1:20 p.m., a total of five minutes. We took off at 12:30 p.m. from Ibsley and arrived promptly on time at our target. We were armed with three 500-pound bombs with 8 to 11-second delay tail fuses, and 12 planes were providing top cover. We crossed the channel and took up our positions and started a sweep across the peninsula.

From classified documents, I learned that this is what we accomplished. Each plane dropped its three 500-pound bombs on railroad tracks, roads, huts, flak guns, and open fields. There was light to heavy flak and small-arms fire as we swept across the peninsula, but our group of P-47s, the most powerful fighter planes in the war, were equipped with eight .50 caliber machine guns and fired 94,280 rounds of armor-piercing, incendiary and tracer ammunition. With that tremendous fire power, Germans must have been ready to surrender. That day, the Ninth Air Force fielded 600 B-26s and A-20s as well as more than 1,200 fighter planes flying and bombing during the day. The main effort was in attacking the Cherbourg peninsula in support of the Seventh Corps assault on the port. Beginning one hour before the ground attack and continuing until the ground assault began, the fighters and bombers pounded the area from low level. As the ground attack began, B-26s and A-6s struck a series of strong points selected by the U.S. First Army, forming a 95-minute aerial barrage. My log shows that our group survived very well except that Second Lt. J. J. Cashman's wing had clipped the tail of Lt. Edward Zeinka's plane. Luckily, the collision was not serious.

I learned later that the German prisoners held in U. S. prisoner of war cages on the ground coined a new catch phrase to describe the allied weapon they feared most, "Jabos," which was short for Jagedebombers. German privates to generals were quoted as saying this was the most terrifying weapon on the western front.

After the mission, I took a long weekend rest and went by train to London. I stayed in one of the Armed Forces-designated hotels and met a lot of guys doing the same thing. Invariably, the Cherbourg assault came up in conversation and after comparing notes, we realized the assaults had been precisely timed and executed five minutes apart.

The city of London was really under siege. At night the German buzz bombs were relentless. My heart went out to the

English people, especially those who were elderly and those with children, many of whom stayed in bomb shelters during the night. One could hear the bombs coming overhead, then a high whining noise and then the explosions. I could only imagine the terror, the destruction and deaths and injuries occurring all over the city, but somehow, life went on for the residents and for me as well. In spite of the war time atmosphere and the destruction, people went about their daily business. I went shopping and found a pretty antique ring for my wife and mailed it off to her.

I was fascinated with what seemed to me the funny little taxicabs. I soon discovered that the funny little taxicabs, which were everywhere, making it simple to get around, were the most civilized cabs ever invented. One could get in, sit down, stretch out one's legs, and have plenty of room overhead.

I took a walk to Piccadilly Circus, where the statues in the center of the square were encased in a wooden structure as protection from the bombings. I also strolled to a narrow street called Jermyn Street, which was lined with what seemed to be very beautiful shops, with the most famous, Fortnum and Mason. Most of the windows of the shops were half empty and some were boarded up.

I found my way to Hyde Park Corner on Brompton Road, and Buckingham Palace, which was exciting for me. Just a short distance from Hyde Park Corner on Brompton Road was the most fabulous department store I had ever seen – Harrod's. Because of my early merchandising training, I found Harrod's fascinating.

My weekend leave was up, and I had to get back to Ibsley. On June 27 Major Morrissey led a flight of 24 P-47s on an armed reconnaissance mission looking for trouble between Laval, Angers, and Nantes. We were flying low across the country with fragmentation clusters, bombs designed to shatter upon impact. We bombed and strafed, leaving massive destruction of more than 50 boxcars burning and exploding. We even caught a large truck, which we destroyed for good measure. The flak and gunfire we ran into were hazardous and some of the planes suffered damage. Our purpose was to make it almost impossible for the Germans to supply their front lines.

I think Hitler was finally beginning to realize that this was the main invasion point and not Calais, which was the port closest to Folkestone, England. On our way back from the June 27 mission, we crossed the lower part of the Cherbourg Peninsula, running into heavy flak again.

On my way back, I was running low on gas, and I told my men to leave me and return to the field. I adjusted my fuel mixture and eased back on the throttle to save gas. In the distance, I saw the Isle of Wight, but at the same time, my red warning light went on. This meant that I had about 40 gallons of gasoline left that would last about 20 minutes flying time. As I flew over the Isle of Wight, I looked for an air field where I could make an emergency landing and get enough gas to get me back to Ibsley. Finding no landing spot on the Isle of Wight, I continued over to the mainland. By now the sun had set and it was beginning to get dark and I knew I didn't have much time left. Finally, I spotted a small grassy landing strip. I realized this must be a landing strip for the English Spitfires – planes small enough to land on short runways. I swung my plane around, and as I approached the runway, they flashed a red warning light for me to go around. I really didn't think I had enough gas to do this, but I didn't know what was happening underneath or behind me, and I thought I might have been getting into more trouble by trying to land. In addition, I had no way of contacting the crew at this field because they used a different radio channel than we did. I went around and came in for another landing, really hitting the bottom of the tank. As I came in low, their warning light went on again, but I had no choice. I searched around and did not see any other planes so I ignored their warning light and landed. I taxied over to the building. Their staff came out, and lots of explanations on my part followed, I told them I needed enough gas to get back to

Ibsley, and soon the smallest gasoline truck I had ever seen pulled up beside my tremendous fighter and began uncoiling a well-worn old-fashioned gas hose. The crew gave me barely enough gasoline to get back to my field, explaining they were obliged to conserve. I had heard that England was feeling the pinch on equipment and supplies, and this experience seemed to prove this.

On June 29, Capt. Moss Fletcher, the operations officer, led the squadron on a bombing mission against gun positions in the Cherbourg City area. The city had been encircled in the last few days by the Allies and was cut off from any help. But the Germans were tough and seemed ready to fight to the bitter end. Our first casualty on this mission was Capt. Fischette, who was hit and forced to pull out. He called on me to make the first run on the target with my flight. We dropped our bombs on the targets and headed home.

The same day one of my fellow flight commanders, Capt. Victor Cabas, led a small mission of nine P-47s to provide cover for the 405th Fighter Bomber Group. This was a really screwed-up mission. Our planes were armed with two fragmentation clusters and one belly tank, but this mission called for two wing tanks and making that change caused us to be 25 minutes late in getting started. Then, when we arrived in France, there was a cloud cover over the area. Between flying below and above the clouds and getting a late start, we ended up providing only five minutes of cover for the 405th. Vic took us down to strafe, however, and we blew up two locomotives. This was sort of a consolation prize, but it still seemed a hell of a way to wind up the month of June.

Two of our squadrons of the 48th already had moved to our new strip in Normandy, and I looked forward to joining them as soon as possible so that we wouldn't have to cross the channel for each mission.

July 3 was our last mission out of Ibsley. I was leading a flight of 11 P-47s, each armed with two 500-pound bombs. The target was an artillery position, and we found the area but when we circled over it, we could not identify any artillery positions. We were flying through low flak during our search. There seemed to be no doubt that the guns were camouflaged so we dove in at a 30-degree angle and dropped our bombs at 2,000 feet. This was one of the frustrating jobs, going after camouflaged guns and troops. The allies had overwhelming superiority, but the Germans often were able to remain invisible from the air. Our troops on the ground, though, could often spot the Germans with binoculars and give us their locations.

I awakened the next morning, July 4, and packed a few last-minute things to carry with me on the move. I left my beloved bike behind and said goodbye to Ibsley and "dear old England." I made a promise to myself that I would return again at a happier time. I had fallen in love with these wonderful, courageous people.

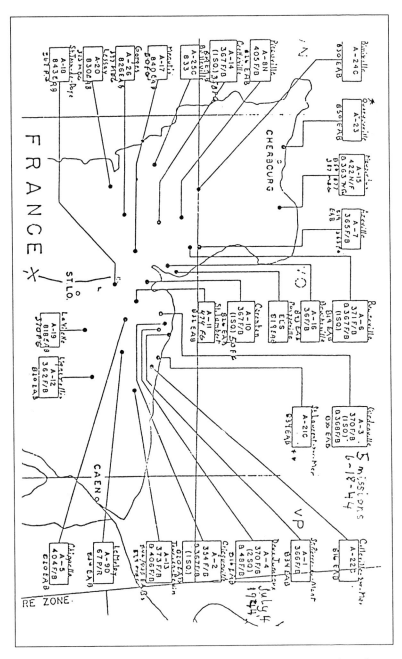

Map of Normandy showing the tremendous build-up of Allied air strips. I flew across the channel with the 48th Fighter Bomber Group, 494th Squadron to our new headquarters in France at Deux-Jumeaux known as A4.

# 10

## The Battle of Normandy

I led my flight across the channel and 45 minutes later we landed at A-4, our new field, which was near the village of Deux-Jumeaux in Northern France. We were just a few miles from Omaha Beach, one of the invasion beaches to the north with the battle line just south of us.

I found my assigned tent and set up my cot and foot locker and with four men of my flight, we started digging fox holes. We made them about a foot deep and just long enough to lie in. I looked around and there were Cabos, Fletcher, Fishette, Morrissey, and some other pilots digging away. Their fox hole was tremendous – at least 7 feet deep – and featuring steps leading to the bottom. It was big enough to hold all of them comfortably.

Here in France there was one rule that was essential to our survival. During the day, the Allied fighters and bombers were to control the air, and Allied ground troops were not to fire at any plane, whether they thought it friend or foe. However, after sunset and as it got dark, our fighter planes were to be safely back at the field. We had learned the hard way in other theaters of operation that too many trigger-happy ground troops had shot down Allied planes because they didn't recognize them as friendly craft. The planes came in so fast and so low, it was impossible for the ground forces to identify them. Since we had such an overwhelming control of the air, it was better that the few German fighters who got through during the day be spared ground fire than that any of our planes be shot down by our own defense.

We were located in a lovely part of Normandy, right in the middle of an apple orchard. One could not ask for a more serene setting.

By the night of July 4, 1944, we were all settled down as if we had been there for a month. The anti-aircraft crews were on duty, and there was sort of a relaxing atmosphere. We turned out the lights and went to sleep – but not for long. With a thundering noise, German fighter planes came barreling through the sky, blazing their guns. At the first sound of attack, I jumped out of my cot and made a beeline for my fox hole. Our anti-aircraft guns opened up with everything they had, and the attack was over as fast as it had begun. It didn't take me long to get back in my cot and go to sleep again.

As time went on, we learned to cope with the German strafing. There were enough air strips in the area that the chances of finding us were pretty slim. Soon, when they did show up, we just rolled over and went back to sleep. Besides, when a German plane came screaming through at 50 feet or lower, he was in and out before we could do anything anyway. The real problem was trying to sleep through the noise of our anti-aircraft fire all around us shooting at these planes.

The next job we tackled was to set up a tent for our bar. I don't remember now whether we brought our bar with us from England or made a new one, but I do remember how important it was for us to gather there to drink and relax. It amazes me now to think how in those days the government thought liquor was so important. We were allowed two ounces of hard liquor after each mission – something like the old days when the British Navy supplied their sailors with rum. If I had actually drunk my allotment on the days when I flew as many as five missions a day, I don't think I could have maneuvered my plane back to the field.

Our flight surgeon, Capt. "Doc" Stone, not only kept us healthy but also kept a tally of our liquor rations and saw to it that we were credited with our proper share at the bar. Those bottles were placed in the bar for any officer and guest to drink as much as he pleased.

Up to that time, almost every mission had been to a location on the map that I could pin down by association with the town to which I had flown. Now, we had a map of a small area of Normandy on which we would be concentrating. That map showed all the towns as well as every large and small road, farm houses and anything visible from the air that would help us locate the target. Printed on the map were coordinate grids with a numbering and lettering system so we could locate any spot in the given area.

After a day of getting settled, Major Morrissey led a flight of 11 to take out a bridge north of Lessay. We overshot the bridge but severed the rail connections between Lessay and the bridge – half a loaf was better than none. It was great not to have to make the round-trip flight over the channel for our missions.

Since I was given the next day off, I grabbed a Jeep and was off to engage in my favorite pastime, playing tourist. I headed for the town of Longueville and La Cambe. Small villages fascinated me, and I had so enjoyed exploring the English hamlets near our Ibsley base. I loved walking the narrow streets and poking around in the small local shops. I bought some foodstuffs that I knew we would enjoy and then headed out on the country roads. I stopped at a farm and bought a whole can of fresh milk, despite the warning we had received that the local milk was not pasteurized.

I drank as much as I could and took the rest back to the base and put it in the bar to share with the fellows. After they had their fill, there was still a lot left over and I didn't want to throw it away. I went to the kitchen for  a flour sack, washed it out and poured the milk into it. I tied a string around the neck of the bag and hung it from an apple tree. I had never done anything like that before but I was experimenting. Several days later I took the bag down and found I had created wonderful-tasting cottage cheese, which was a treat in our wartime diet.

On July 8, Capt. John W. Watson led a flight of 12 of us on a mission to dive bomb a command post. The target was a large gray house at grid #T223582, and we knew that this mission was a request from the troops at the front. Seven 500-pound bombs were dropped on the target, five of which were direct hits.

On the following day Vic Cabas led our flight of 12 on a reconnaissance mission in the Tessy and Benny Bocage area. Bombs were dropped on road junctions and bridges. Those missions must have raised havoc with the German troop movements.

The next few days were spent in routine troop support bombing and strafing missions. Inevitably, though, the thing we feared did happen. Second Lt. Richard Williams, a member of my flight, was hit, while on mission, by friendly anti-aircraft fire. He made it down to an air strip, and luckily he was uninjured.

In another incident, Vic Cabos was on a mission led by our commanding officer, Morrissey. They were flying at 5,000 feet, only 10 minutes away from our field. They were searching for a tank battle near the beachhead area when Vic spotted tanks going in through a hedgerow and made the first run. He skip-bombed from 50 feet using a bomb with a delayed fuse, but he was hit by 20-millimeter guns as he pulled up.

He was hesitant to fly out over the channel because the Germans were still firing at him. He was about to bail out and had one foot on the wing when he spotted a small 2,000-foot runway. He pulled back into the plane and dove to the end of the runway just as his engine died. He was able to land in one piece. He told me that a doctor came up to check him out, found him okay and gave him two shots of scotch This was not a new experience for Vic because he had been shot down in the African campaign before he came to England.

Captain Fischette took the next mission on July 12. This was to hit a railroad bridge with 500-pound bombs from an altitude of 400 feet. We hit with a great pattern on the bridge with one bomb directly in the middle, leaving the target destroyed. A large building nearby was left in flames, and brick barracks, with troops around them were strafed. We met heavy intense flak during the reconnaissance in the area we had covered.

The town of Bayeux had been captured on June 9, three days after the invasion, by the combined forces of the English and Americans. Fortunately, it was taken without damage. Only 18 miles to the east was the city of Caen in the British sector. The British had put tremendous pressure on the Germans to break out of this area, and the city suffered a great deal of damage. The German high command had thrown every bit of armor into the battle for that city.

A few days later I took a Jeep over to Bayeux and found the town was beginning to get back to normal after suffering the trials and tribulations of being under the heels of Nazi dominance. Shops had re-opened and tensions were easing.

It was a lovely ancient city and my first taste of what beautiful old French buildings looked like. I found a small shop selling ladies wear and bought my wife a beautiful silk scarf.

At the same time, the Americans were taking the vital seaport city of Cherbourg.

Caen was finally taken by the allies. I knew what a struggle that had been and did not want to visit that city.

Most of the pilots spent their days off roaming the countryside, but two of them, Lts. R. L. Duel and Milbern A. Quintana, asked for permission to go up to the front lines. They were supposed to come back the same day, but they did not return. No one could find out what had happened to them, and eventually they were given up for lost. Finally, they showed up on August 1. They had made some wrong turns and had been captured by the Germans, but they managed to escape with help from the French Underground. They were not much worse for wear, but certainly much wiser. The sad ending to the story, though, was that on October 28 Quintana was hit with heavy flak while on a mission. His plane was on fire, but he was able to make it back to friendly territory. He rolled his plane over on its back and bailed out, but his parachute never opened. He had been hit by the tail of his plane and knocked unconscious.

Johnny Staring and I took turns on the missions scheduled for our flights to fly. This was during the period that General Patton's "Operation Cobra" was just beginning – this was the breakout from Normandy to sweep across France to Paris.

Three missions we made between July 16 and July 20 were concentrated bombing and strafing of block houses, troops, vehicles, and targets of opportunity. The weather was very poor on some of the flights, with rain, lightning, and electrical storms.

The next time I had leave, I took a Jeep and drove west toward Cherbourg, driving through some small towns that had taken quite a beating during the invasion. As I came to the town of Isigny-s-Mer, I could see the effects of our relentless efforts to capture it. Most of the buildings had been destroyed, and bulldozers had gone through and pushed the debris aside, making a narrow road for traffic. Abruptly, I was waved over to the side and told to stop. Suddenly I heard the noise of oncoming tanks, lots of them making their way along the narrow makeshift road. I looked up and sitting in the lead tank in the turret was none other then General "Blood and Guts" Patton. He was wearing his combat helmet and looking straight ahead with his back rigid, arms folded across his chest, and chin out. I caught a glimpse of his pearl-handled revolver in a holster at his waist. What a sight – the determined look on his face showed he was on his way to take us to Paris in short time.

After the tanks went past, I continued on through Carentan, which also had taken quite a bit of damage during the battle. Swinging north I went through Ste. Mere-Eglise and on up to Cherbourg. It was very exciting to be driving about this, the largest city to be taken by the Allies so far in the war. Poking around, I came to a large tunnel that had been excavated into a hillside. There were a lot of soldiers guarding the place, and I stopped and went in. I could tell this had been a center for the German command. On the walls were racks that had held torpedoes, probably to be put on submarines that may have been docked there, ready to take off for the English Channel. I thought I'd find some souvenirs, but everything had been dismantled by the time I got there.

I headed back to the base, taking the road toward St. Lo. I was getting fairly close to the front lines, and as I passed through a small village, I noticed a burned out Jeep with a figure in the front seat, all burned to a crisp. At first I thought it was a Frenchman, maybe a policeman, because it looked like there was a flat-top uniform hat on his head. But then I realized it was an American G.I. caught in the crossfire a few minutes earlier and the top of his head had been sliced off. I thought then that as a fighter pilot, I was spared the ugly ravages of ground warfare.

On my various jaunts I had bought sugar and gasoline so that I could trade those much-needed items with the French for some of their wines and liqueurs for our bar.

I came to a bombed out building and stopped to examine it. It had been a dairy, and one of the walls inside was covered with 6-inch blue and white tiles, pictures of cows grazing in a meadow. I pried a few off the wall and sent them home as souvenirs from Normandy.

St. Lo, which had been taken by July 18, had been very important for the Germans because it had five roads radiating out from the center of the city, leading in all directions. With the capture of St. Lo, our troops were now able to move to the north, south, east, and west. Patton's tanks were moving so fast and so far that we could envision him spearheading his forces to Paris within a month. However, on some missions south and east of St. Lo, I found it difficult to find tanks and trucks or other enemy targets to take out. They must have been well camouflaged and moving out at night.

On July 24, Colonel Wertenbaker led the group of 36 P-

47s in "Operation Cobra." We each had been armed with four 260-pound fragmentation bombs. We dropped our bombs on the designated area, but because of poor visibility and the fact there were so many planes involved, all attention was given to keeping formation. This was a blanket bombing mission going after German troops, and we encountered heavy flak over the target.

It had been demonstrated that photo reconnaissance and ground source reports were the best means of determining the accuracy of bombing and strafing missions. We pilots were handicapped in the appraisal of damage done by our attacks because of the speed of flight, altitude, smoke, and debris. Intense flak concentrations frequently made it unwise to return to the site to make a visual assessment at low altitude. Our group had very few photos showing our results – something of a disappointment but one we had to live with.

The next day Major Morrissey led us on the same size mission with the same fragmentation bombs. Again we could understand the Germans' fear of the P-47 "Jabos" strafing bombing missions.

Col. Dixon Allison, our first 48th Group C.O., Col. George Wertenbakerh
who took over as Group C.O. and on the right
Gen. General Elwood R. "Pete" Quasada the Commander of the 9th Air Force.

On a day I will never forget, I was among the crowd of officers and enlisted men who packed into a large meadow waiting to see an important visitor. A staff car pulled up and out came General Dwight Eisenhower who had come to visit our base. General Eisenhower strolled down a path about eight feet wide running through the middle of the crowd, shaking hands with as many men as he could touch. It was a thrill to see the man who had made the decision leading to the fantastic invasion.

On another evening there was a less cheerful experience. We were standing around just after sunset. There was still a little light in the sky and we spotted a plane coming toward the beachhead area from the east. It was, of course, against all regulations for an American plane to be flying at night over the battle field, but as it got closer it was unmistakably a P-38. As it flew over our heads, our anti-aircraft opened fire and blew the plane out of the sky. We had no way of knowing if the P-38 had been captured by the Germans, restored and used as camouflage to attack our lines.

During July, one of my men, Dick Williams, ran into trouble. He was flying with Johnny Staring and after completing a 180-degree turn called by his flight leader, he saw another P-47 coming at him head-on. So he pushed everything forward and went into a dive, but when he tried to pull out, he went into a high-speed stall and mushed into some trees, damaging the leading edges of both wings. His engine was running rough and losing oil, but he managed to climb to 1,000 feet and drop his bomb. Coming back over friendly territory, he was met by flak and small arms fire. He opened his canopy and started to climb out but realized he was too low; so he clambered back into his plane and bellied it in. He was not injured and was awarded membership in the "Late Arrival Club."

Our well stocked bar in our new
French Quarters. We were credited
with 2 ounces for every mission.

A favorite meeting place –
Adam, Fischette, Cabas, Orwatt, Morrissey, Snetting and Van Risswick.

# 11

## In "The Thick of It"

By July 27, the ground forces were making fantastic gains south of St. Lo and Coutances. Patton was leading his forces in an end run to the south, searching for any German forces, tanks, trucks, or other enemy vehicles moving around the side roads. Our 48th Group started flying in the morning and sent out five missions during the day. The Germans were fleeing, barely running ahead of the Combat Team B of the Third Armored division. It was a real rout in the area of Cerisy and Canisy, but there were battles going on all over the sector. Vic Cabas led one mission in which a pilot, Lt. E. T. Jones, was hit by flak and had to make a crash landing. He was not injured. Dick Morrissey, who had been promoted to deputy group commander, led another mission.

My mission that day was one of the last in the afternoon. It included more bombing, strafing, and raising hell with the retreating German forces. As I was heading north to home base, I was flying low looking for anything to shoot at. I was no more than 100 to 150 feet high when I saw a village ahead of me that had been almost completely destroyed. I pushed the nose of my plane down and flew down the main street, looking to the left and right at the stone buildings that had been reduced to rubble. As I left the town, I pulled up to about 500 feet and headed north to my base. Suddenly, I ran into a wall of machine gun fire, and I felt my plane shudder from the impact. My engine started sputtering and I fought to keep on course. My windshield was thick with oil as my engine had been hit. I shoved my stick forward, nosing down to get to the level of trees and bushes and to get out of the range of the guns. I knew if I got low enough, I could get out of there before they could hit me. I stayed down low, working my way through the trees until I was sure I was over the front lines and into friendly territory. Then I realized I was in real trouble and possibly couldn't make it back. I contacted my field, calling out, "May Day, May Day. I'll try to make it back." At first, I did not get an answer, but then I called again and identified myself. They had gotten my message and they said that the field would be cleared for me to come in. I climbed to about 500 feet, keeping my eyes open for an emergency landing if necessary. My engine was running very rough, and there wasn't much chance to making it back. Suddenly, I spotted the field just ahead of me. It was very late in the evening, and I was just barely ahead of the time when American anti-aircraft lines would open up on me.

I was slowly losing altitude as the field came closer, and I had barely touched down at the end of the runway when my engine died. My concern now was to get my plane out of the way for any pilots behind me coming in from the mission. As soon as I slowed down, I turned off the runway onto the grass. With a sigh of relief, I climbed out of the cockpit and was greeted by my fellow pilots.

There was no doubt in my mind that the ground support was the most dangerous part of flying in combat. Flying low as we had to do, we not only were subjected to anti-aircraft fire but also we were target practice for every German with a rifle. I had returned to the base with my plane shot full of shrapnel and bullet holes. By then it was dark and I went in to give a full report of the mission.

The next day I went out to see my crew chief to find out what condition my plane was in for my next mission. Unfortunately, there was a lot of work to be done. Twenty millimeter shells had exploded in the engine and on the wing, and I had been lucky to have made it back in one piece. Only the rugged P-47 could have taken this beating and taken me home. Now it needed a new engine. I was not scheduled to fly until three days later, July 30.

The next day the pilots returning from their mission reported that one of them, Lt. Frederick Larner, had been forced to bail out over enemy territory and his plane had been destroyed by his own bomb fragments.

I had scheduled Johnny Staring to lead the mission on July 30. When I woke up that morning, I went to see what the mission orders were. I had never seen so many orders developing for the day, but due to weather conditions, most were for afternoon missions. This was the schedule for the 48th Group: the 492nd Squadron was scheduled for nine missions as was the 493rd with my 494th Squadron scheduled for seven missions. "Cobra Operation" was now in full swing. My Flight D was scheduled to take off at 2:45 p.m. and land at 3:24 p.m. All the bombing and strafing missions were to be done in advance of the troop line from the coast to about 30 miles inland on the Cherbourg Peninsula. For the first time, we were going to experiment with 45-second delay fuses, and this would call for new tactics in bombing.

I could see in advance that this was going to be one of our most exciting missions and I hated to miss it. I called Johnny over and said, "Buddy, I hate to do this to you, but this sounds like a really good mission and I'd like to take this for myself." With that, I erased his name and put mine in his place. There were four of us in that flight – Woody Klinner, my wing man; Edward "Zink" Zeinka and his wing man, whose name I don't remember. Our planes were loaded up with two 500-pound bombs with the new 45-second delay fuses. The theory was that we could come down on a tank, drop a bomb and have 45 seconds to get away before the explosion.

Since the actual dive bombing had begun only on March

93

15, 1944, with the formation of the Ninth Tactical fighters, and the real ground support had begun on D-Day, June 6, none of us were very experienced at this kind of combat. We were all learning the hard way.

We took off at 2:45 p.m. and flew south to the road between Percy and Granville on the coast.

We had no trouble locating the German tanks on the road that were our targets. I alerted my men to keep in close radio contact because we didn't want to come down on a tank that was about to blow up under us. The 45-second delay could be a very tricky thing, and also, it could malfunction and go off too early or too late.

I peeled off and came in low just a few feet above the tank and dropped a bomb right under the treads. Then I pulled up and circled around. Below I could see the tank moving away from the bomb before it went off. Damn it. We hadn't counted on this.

One after another, my men did the same thing and each time the tank had plenty of time to move away before the damn bomb went off. Then I told my men to hold up the bombing while I went down and machine-gunned the treads so that the tank couldn't move.

I thought that eight 50-caliber machine guns would be able to put the tank out of commission, and I came in low, 10 feet off the ground and fired a long burst. As I pulled up over the tank, a bomb went off under my plane. There must have been a faulty fuse and I had caught it. My plane was thrown into the air and oil spattered everywhere. I figured I was in trouble, but as I pulled up and around and checked my instruments, everything seemed to be fine. The only problem was that the windshield was covered with oil. I was determined to get the tank and I alerted the rest of the flight, telling them to hold off until I had dropped my last bomb. My engine was running smoothly now, and I swung around for another approach so that I could put the bomb right in the middle of the tank. I came in , blazing with my guns wide open and dropped my bomb right under the tread of the tank. There was no way he could get away this time. At the same moment as I fired my guns and dropped my bomb, bullets hit my plane. I couldn't have been more than 10 feet off the ground as I went over the tank when my engine burst into flames and the plane became a flying torch.

Behind the tank on the road was a hill, and I pulled my stick back to try to gain altitude,. I realized I had to get out of the plane fast. The flames were a solid mass around me but were kept out of the cockpit by the closed canopy. At about 500 feet, I opened my canopy and with that, the flames swept in and almost enveloped me. I pushed up to get out and then realized I hadn't released my safety belt. I ducked down out of the flames, released the belt and pushed out. As I got out on the right side, flames began to lick at me. I went through intense heat, fanned by oil from the engine., But there was no time for fear, no time for hesitation, only time for action. The second I was clear of the plane, I pulled my rip cord and felt a jerk. I didn't have time to look to see if my chute had opened before my feet hit the ground.

EPILOGUE: OFFICIAL RECORDS OF MY LAST MISSION OF THE 48TH FIGHTER BOMBER GROUP

The 48th Fighter Bomber Group, consisting of 48 P-47s, had completed 25 missions that day. The group had used 196 500-pound bombs, 54 with the regular eight to 11-second fuses, and 194 with the new 45-second delay fuses. The results of our group mission for the day were 23 tanks and 40 vehicles destroyed and another 38 damaged and probably destroyed. Bridges, defended houses, and railroad tracks also were strafed and bombed.

Our aircraft suffered severe damage from flak as follows: Three aircraft and pilots missing – Capt. Mozart Kaufman, Lt. Woody R. Klinner Jr. and Lt. Anton G. Von Risswick. Lt. Von Risswick was seen parachuting down into friendly territory and returned to the base that afternoon. Thirteen aircraft were damaged by flak, one flying through a tree, and another suffering a punctured tire, which caused the plane to nose-over on landing.

# 12

## Suddenly I'm a POW

I immediately had a few quick thoughts about making escape plans as I unbuckled my parachute and looked around for a direction to run.

When I started up the hill, a German soldier came running down toward me with a drawn Luger pistol. He was such a pipsqueak of a guy, a little fellow with wire-rimmed glasses and a pinched, nervous look. I was tempted to take him on and fight my way out of this spot, but the Luger was such a neutralizer that fighting him was only a fleeting thought. I put my hands up, and he directed me to walk up the hill to a small one-man building outpost. We were not very far behind the front lines, and I knew our forces were moving very fast under Patton's command. It seemed very quiet and peaceful there, but I knew all hell was breaking loose just over the hill.

I thought that if we stayed there long enough, our troops were bound to appear and my troubles would be over. At that point, however, I realized I was badly burned and needed medical attention. I opened my escape and first aid kit, looking for medicine. I found some sulfa drugs, which I applied to the burns on both my wrists and face and around my eyes. I indicated to the soldier that I needed a doctor. There didn't seem to be anyone else around, but finally, after some time, another soldier appeared, and I was taken in his motorcycle side-car across country to the rear of the battle zone.

On the trip the soldier was forced to stop many times and pull over under a tree because of fighter planes sweeping the area. I then realized where all the Germans had been hiding when I was flying and looking for targets.

We finally came to a very large tent that seemed to be a command center. Several hours after my crash, a doctor and a first aid man showed up. As they started treating my burns, I realized for the first time that I was not only burned around my eyes and on my wrists but also on my neck, arms, and back. My goggles had saved my eyes, and my oxygen mask had saved my nose and mouth. My chamois gloves had shrunk up at the moment the flames hit them and left my wrists below my sleeves unprotected, and both the arm and back of my jacket were burned through to my skin.

After being treated, I was joined by an American sergeant who had just been captured, and we were marched to a farmhouse about five miles away. We were searched and shown to our quarters for the night – an old stall with hay on the ground. There was no water or food, so we settled down to a cold restless night. After an hour or so, I woke up with a chill. My teeth started chattering and my whole body began shaking. I was cold from the shock of the burns, and I would have given anything for a warm blanket. For the rest of the night I was awake, shaking and shuddering.

All during the night and the next day, our numbers kept increasing as captured infantrymen were brought there. At noon on July 31, 1944, we received a bowl of soup, our only meal of the day. That night we were loaded into a truck with seats on both sides of the back. So many soldiers were packed into the middle that the seated men had no room on the floor for their feet. Since I was the only casualty, my fellow prisoners insisted that I have a seat. I also was the only officer and a fighter pilot who may have given these troops ground support.

On August 1 at 4:00 in the morning, we were still rolling through the French countryside when I realized I had a big problem. Nature had been calling, and there was no way to delay any longer. Luckily, I had a small roll of toilet paper in my shirt pocket that I carried for just such an emergency. I made my way over everyone's feet to the tailgate of the truck and sat next to the German guard with my back end hanging out over the tailgate and my feet and legs stretched over the large German police dog that was guarding us. The dog did not move, which indicated to me that he was trained to respond only to commands. I did my duty and returned to my seat in the truck. Once I showed this could be done without getting shot or chewed up, many of the other men followed my example.

At dawn we pulled up to a farmyard, where the French people were very kind to us. They brought us bread, butter, hard-boiled eggs, and chicken salad. However, by then, my burns were getting very painful, and I had little appetite for food.

During that day I made my first plans to escape. The back of the building was unguarded, and I forced the back door and had it ready to open. I was already to escape as soon as it became dark, but luck was against me as we started on another crowded ride at dusk.

The next day, August 2, we arrived in the early morning at a prison camp at Alençon, and we were shoved into a large barracks for the night. There were double bunk beds with three narrow boards on each bed stretched from head to foot. This left a choice of which narrow board on which to sleep, and I found they all hurt. There was much groaning and snoring and very little sleep for anyone. As soon as there was a streak of light in the sky, we started stirring and stretching our legs. The next problem was that we were locked up in a dirt floor barracks with no toilet facilities. At this point, some of the soldiers realized they no longer needed their helmets for combat, so they used them as toilets.

At 8:00 a.m. we were given our ration – a small amount of black bread with a touch of jam and some ersatz coffee. A thorough search followed the meal, and then we were moved to another barracks where there were straw mattresses on the bunks, a big improvement over the other facility. The morning bread ration was all the food we were given until evening, when we received a bowl of watery soup. Our days of hunger had begun.

On August 3, I spent the entire day trying to get medical attention. Every promise for treatment was cancelled at the last minute. I finally located an American first aid man and talked him into changing my bandage so my burns wouldn't get infected.

The next day at 1:00 p.m. we were jammed into trucks again, and we arrived in Chartres at 6:00 in the evening. There, we were taken to a large prison, where the flight officers were separated from the infantrymen. After several hours, we fliers were turned over to the Luftwaffe and marched across town to a large Catholic complex. Here we were placed in a big room with straw scattered on the floor for bedding.

We stayed in the same building for the next three days, but on August 6, there was a thorough search and then we were moved to another room, where a couple of bales of hay were given to us to spread on the floor. For toilet facilities, we were escorted outside to a courtyard where there was an 8-foot deep hole with a log along one side. The only advantage was that there were large leafy trees nearby and we had built-in toilet paper. Every day more airmen were added to our numbers, and by August 8, there were 59 of us.

In the early hours of August 10, we were loaded into three small trucks to begin another ride, arriving in Paris at 7:00 a.m. I had been looking forward to my arrival in Paris ever since leaving America, but this was the most depressing entry to the city I could ever have imagined. We drove through the almost deserted streets in the early morning, looking in vain for some of the famous landmarks. We were taken to the railroad station in the middle of the city and were marched to a second floor room where there were 59 cots lined up against the wall for our next stay.

From August 9 to August 15, we were in this small room

with half-circle windows low to the floor. We were able to look out onto the station below where the trains arrived and departed, and we watched as thousands of German soldiers and their families fleeing the city. We realized that General Patton and his tanks must not be far away, but for us, it could have been 1,000 miles for all the good it did us.

During the day the French Red Cross brought us food. I asked if there was a place to have my burns cared for, and they told me that there was a first aid station in the building. The next day a guard took me out and we walked the full length of the station until I saw a lighted glass ball with a white cross on a green background. I was taken inside, and a very nice French nurse with a stiff white starched hat was waiting for me.

She unwrapped the bandages on my wrist and picked up a flask with a pointed curved end on the top. She turned it over my wrist, and rubbing alcohol poured out onto my burns. Then I knew what real pain was, but I felt I couldn't let this nice lady know what she was doing to me; so I just clinched my teeth and didn't flinch. She then went over to a dish, picked up a small plum and popped it into my mouth. It was the most delicious thing I had tasted since July 30.

As I was being marched back to the other end of the station, I felt very cocky walking among all the German soldiers. I knew they were licked even if they didn't know it yet, and I knew they were running like scared rabbits.

Back in my room with my buddies, I showed off the plum pit, and they were all jealous of me. Such a little thing meant so much – when food is scarce, one's idea of what is important changes very fast.

Two days later, the nurse came back and asked the guard to bring me to her office to have my dressing changed again. It was a hard decision to make. I thought about the rubbing alcohol and the plum, and I must admit, the plum won out. Back I went to the other end of the station, the alcohol treatment and a plum in my mouth again. It seemed worth it, and all I could say was, "merci beaucoup."

On August 9 as we were ready to leave Paris, we were asked to sign a paper promising not to attempt to escape if we were under attack during the train trip. If we signed the paper, we would be allowed to leave the train during Allied air attacks and run for cover. All of us refused to sign, reserving our rights under the Geneva Convention for prisoners of war to attempt to escape. At 6:00 in the evening, we were taken to a train, where one car had been reserved for us. The other cars were occupied by German troops and families fleeing Paris.

As we were being loaded onto the train, the German sergeant checked us off by name. When he came to Mozart Kaufman, he approached me and said, "Jewish." I told him I was, and he then said Kaufman meant "merchant" in German. I waited for something else to follow, but that was the end of the conversation.

We were divided up among the compartments and even though it was crowded, we were able to get along all right during the day. Night was the problem – everyone began stretching out on the floor, trying to find comfortable places to sleep.

I was determined to escape before the train left France, and on the first night I took a seat next to the window. When it became dark and the lights had been turned down in the compartments, I started slowly raising the window. The window movement was noisy, and I only raised it a fraction of an inch at a time, keeping an eye out for the guard who was constantly checking us. Although it was very nerve-wracking, by midnight I had the window up about 12 inches. It was then I realized that the guard was watching me because I could see the outline of the side of his face just slightly peering into the window of the door. I then realized I was taking a chance of being shot if I slipped out the window, and I very slowly started closing it. I had it closed in about an hour, but I was so strung out over my failure to escape that I gave up any thought of sleep for the rest of the night.

The next day we were attacked by P-38s. The train had come to a stop just before the attack, and all the Germans from the full length of the train dashed into the woods. Before the guards left us, they told us to keep our heads down out of sight or they would shoot us from the woods. The train was strafed, but luckily, none of us were hit. In fact, I don't even remember any bullets coming into our coach. But it was terrifying being attacked while penned up this way; men were screaming all around me.

When the P-38s left, the Germans poured back onto the train and we started off again. The sergeant then offered us another chance to sign the paper entitling us to leave the train in case of another air attack. There was a great deal of argument and I tried to convince my fellow officers that we should not sign. But 58 men signed – I was the only hold-out. I was determined to keep my option to escape if I had any chance at all and I thought that with the likelihood of bombings and more strafing, I stood a good chance.

The German sergeant then laid down the rules for me in case of more attacks. I must stand in front of a window facing the soldiers in the woods, and one soldier would be assigned to train his rifle on me. If I even lowered my hands, I would be shot. I told him I understood. For the next five days, we had two or three evacuations a day from the train with everyone, including my fellow prisoners, dashing into the safety of the woods. I did as I was told and stood with my arms raised high with the bandages covering the burns. I don't remember feeling any pain, probably because I was so glad to be challenging those damn Germans.

Nights were the hardest part of the trip because there was no place to sleep comfortably. The second night after my botched escape attempt, I climbed up on the luggage rack, which consisted of three pieces of brass coming out from the wall, one on each end and one in the middle connected to a rod running the full length. This had a heavy fish net material strung over it. It was difficult enough to climb up to it but when stretched out, the only real support was the brass rod across the middle. but I was alone without anyone squirming around on top of me. In addition to this, the food and water rations on the trip were at an absolute minimum.

On August 15, we arrived at Frankfurt, where the train made a stop at the station. It took us five days on the train to cover a distance that today's travelers can make in eight and a half hours – the difference, of course, were the numerous attacks by Allied planes. In Frankfurt, everywhere we looked, there was total destruction. It seemed amazing that the train could even pull into the station because of the devastation. In the station, the guards made us pull down the shades after the civilians realized who we were.

We stayed on the train which then went on to Bad Homburg, 10 miles north of Frankfurt. When we left the train there, we were very weak from short rations and cramped quarters.

We were now at the Dulag Luft Interrogation Center, where we were searched again and taken to solitary confinement cells. The cells were about 6 feet by 9 feet, with a wooden pallet and straw mattress, a stool, and a water bottle in each. After the long train ride, it was very special to have water any time I wanted it.

Dulag Luft, near Frankfurt, the interrogation center for Allied Air Force Officers shot down. This center was used by the Allies holding German scientists after the war. My records show that some of these German scientists ended up in the United States.

In a short time, a guard came and took me to be interrogated by a man named Hanns Scharff. I thought at the time that he was an officer, but he had no rank showing, and I learned much later that he was a non-commissioned officer. He started off in a low-key manner, asking the usual questions. I told him my name, rank, and serial number, and said that was all I was going to tell him. He then proceeded to try to get additional information in a round-about way, with no luck. He also mentioned the fact that I was Jewish but did not try to threaten me with this. Finally, he dismissed me and sent me back to my cell, where I was to remain for 30 days because I refused to give any information.

Life in solitary turned out to be a monotonous and dreary confinement. To make matters worse, the food rations were kept to an absolute minimum. It was a continuation of the starvation diet we had had for the past two weeks, only more so. I received two thin slices of heavy black bread with a touch of ersatz jam for breakfast. Lunch consisted of a cup of watery soup, and for dinner, there were two more thin slices of black bread with a bit of margarine and a cup of ersatz tea that I passed up. Without exercise, this diet would have kept me alive for quite some time, but I was hoping it would not come to that.

Hanns Scharff, my German interrogator at Dulag Luft. Many years after the war he had become an American citizen in California and a famous mosaic artist. We became friends and he sent me this photo. He died September 10, 1992 in Bear Valley Springs, California.

This is what it was like for me in solitary confinement
at Dulag Luft.

Hanns Scharff (second from right), the former German interrogator, and
Raymond Tolliver (far right), author of "The Interrogator," at the P47
Thunderbolt Pilots Assoication gathering in San Diego, May 1987.

After dinner, the shutters were closed at 8 p.m. and the lights turned out for a long night of thinking and dreaming about everything I would like to be doing. At 7:30 a.m. the shutters were opened, but the windows were frosted, and we were unable to see what was going on outside. However, I don't remember ever being frightened about what was happening to me. I just took one day at a time and didn't worry about the future.

I was not completely without company for those days – the cell was full of fleas, and it became a game killing them. I was tempted to keep score, but I realized after a short time that the numbers would run too high and it would be boring.

We were warned not to deface the walls under any condition, although I wondered what additional punishment they would inflict on me. I had a safety pin or something sharp because I made a small scratch on the wall very low near the bed where I could see it when I opened my eyes each morning. This was the way I kept track of my days in solitary confinement.

# 13

## Solitary and Interrogation

I heard more prisoners being brought in and taken out each day, but I never tried to talk to them because I had no way of knowing if they were "plants" to try to gain information.

On August 17 and 18 the interrogation by Hanns Scharff continued. He was a very smart questioner who used low-key methods to extract information, no matter how insignificant. He tried to talk to me about home and family, anything to pick up bits of information that could be useful when the next pilot came through from my outfit. With the next man, he could then casually mention things I had talked about to show that such conversation was all right. Then he would start fishing for the date he really wanted. In an attempt to show me how foolish I was for refusing to talk, he asked me how many states there were in the union. I replied, "sorry, but only name, rank, and serial number." I was so intent on not revealing anything more that I didn't realize until later that he wanted to see if I had any reaction if I answered "48," because I was in the 48th Fighter Bomber group.

On August 20, I was interrogated again in a repeat of the earlier sessions. However, this turned out to be different. Afterward, Hanns Scharff allowed me to clean up for the first time in three weeks. I was given a small piece of ersatz soap, a dull razor blade, and some terrible shaving soap. The soap melted away before my eyes, but just getting water to wash the dirt away helped. The razor and shaving soap were another matter, but I was able to scrape the three-week beard off my face.

Then I had another surprise. I was to be allowed to go to the library and I read a book a day until I left the interrogation center. I read books like "Yankee Lawyer," "The Robe," "Goodbye, Mr. Chips," "The Devil and Daniel Webster," "Cimmarron," and many others. Some of them struck my fancy and others even though I was hungry for entertainment, were awful.

On August 28 I was marched out of solitary with 40 other prisoners and taken to a shower for de-lousing. Again I was given a piece of soap that melted in moments, but to be under a shower for the first time in 29 days was a real treat. As we marched to the showers, I noticed there were cabbages planted around the barracks area. When we were marched back, I positioned myself in the middle of the group and at just the right moment, I stepped into the garden, snatched up one of the scrawny cabbages and put it in my shirt. I was not spotted, and I made it back to my room free and clear. What a treat that cabbage was! I don't ever remember tasting anything so delicious.

The de-lousing, however, turned out to have been a waste of time. The fleas were in the straw, and I killed six of them the very next day.

On August 29, I had another interrogation with no success for Hanns Scharff. At 8 p.m. the shutters were closed as usual but about one or two hours later, my door was opened by a guard and I was taken back to Hanns Scharff.

When I entered his office, he told me that this was not going to be an interrogation session but just a time for us to sit and relax and have a drink together. I told Hanns that I didn't want to do this alone but that if he would bring another American officer to join us, I would be glad to chat with him. He sent for another officer, a captain, who joined us and then I laid down the ground rules for our social gathering. I said we could not discuss anything to do with matters outside of Germany, including anything regarding America, whether it was family, politics, or history, or any other polite conversation topics.

I said I would be willing to discuss anything on this side of the German border including his family, the German people or Hitler. I said I would be glad to tell him exactly what I thought of Hitler. I was a little surprised to have him agree that perhaps there were things to be said about Hitler. Then I realized he would talk about Germany or Hitler as long as he could use the subjects to try to pry information out of me.

With that, the party started and he served us a very good French brandy in nice liqueur glasses topped off with a thick cream which I could only compare to the best English Devonshire cream. With the subject-matter limited to my rules, we proceeded to have a very nice social conversation and a pleasant evening.

The conversation was going well even when I told him in no uncertain words what I thought of Hitler. He didn't bat an eyelash, and we continued talking with Scharff trying every once in awhile to steer the talk to America. Whether the question was aimed at me or my fellow prisoner, I would stop the conversation.

In the next hour and a half or two hours, we must have had four to six of these potent drinks, but amazingly, I felt no effects from the brandy. Finally, Hanns bid us good night and we returned to our cells. I awoke the next morning feeling fine with no after-effects from the brandy or the "Devonshire cream."

The next day brought another interrogation session, but still no information on my end. I felt Hanns Scharff should be giving up soon. He was a very clever interrogator. He kept jabbing at me from different directions and questions and general conversation to draw me around to the things he really wanted to find out. I was very careful to keep a poker face so that when he hit a sensitive point, I didn't show any surprise in my expression. It was a real cat and mouse game, even though a deadly one.

By September 13, I had been cooling my backside for a long time even though I had enjoyed reading the books from the library. Surely this period should be coming to an end soon. I heard hundreds of prisoners come and go for the last month. I wondered what they were doing that was different. Certainly, they were not blabbing. (After the war, however, I learned that Hanns Scharff claimed to have gotten some form of information from at least 96 percent of the prisoners he interrogated.)

On September 14, I was ushered in for another interrogation, but after a few minutes of attempting to obtain information from me, I was told that they knew all about me and that my holding out for the last month was a waste of effort on my part. Hanns Scharff told me I was in the 48th Group, 494th Squadron, and then he told me when I had arrived in England and many more of the details he had been pressuring me for. He then laid out before me the actual orders bringing me from America to England, and he showed me the cut orders listing the code words we used to identify ourselves when using the radio on combat mission. This list was not only for our squadron, but for several groups. I had not seen these papers although some of them apparently were in my file at headquarters.

Now the interrogation started all over again with him trying to get me to admit to these facts. I think I must have surprised him because I not only would not acknowledge any of the papers, but I still would not give him anything but my name, rank, and serial number. I still felt very strongly that to admit anything further would just break the dike and open the way for him to learn what he needed to fill in the puzzle.

After more attempts to get me to say more or to show some expression, he finally asked me if I would like a bowl of noodles. Naturally, my answer was yes and an orderly brought in a large bowl of noodles which I consumed in record time.

He then asked if I would like another serving and a second bowl was brought to me and eaten just as fast. This was more food than I had eaten at any one time in the past month and a half. Then I received the good news that I was being released from solitary confinement. I was returned to my cell, but before the day was over, I was moved to another building where there were other officers.

It was hard to believe that I was able to move about freely and talk to my fellow officers. But I became defensive again, afraid that a German had been put into our group to gain the last bit of information we had not revealed to Scharff.

I listened and made general conversation, but would not discuss military matters of any type.

For dinner, we received regular food, and sitting around the table talking with friends made me realize how much we took for granted.

During the night I began to pay for the pleasure of eating normally for the first time, as diarrhea struck me with the force of a sledge hammer.

On September 15, a large group of us marched out, leaving Dulag Luft forever and taking a train to Wertzal. There we received an even more wonderful surprise. We were walked through a line and given a Red Cross parcel filled with delicious things from home – canned fruit, meat and fish, Vitamin D-fortified chocolate bars, cookies and cigarettes, which I used for bargaining money since I didn't smoke. Down the line we were given new clean army shirts, pants, underwear, socks, towels, and even a wash cloth. But the best was yet to come. It almost brought tears to my eyes to see a tooth brush, tooth paste, and real American soap. How could I have fought taking baths when I was a little boy? This was heaven.

We were led to showers where the water came pouring out hot, and with the wash cloth I slathered the soap all over me. After a month and a half, there was much dirt to wash off, and the tooth brush also was worked overtime.

Then in a glow of happiness, we were led to a room and given special printed paper on which to write home telling our families we were well. The guard even told us that those letters to our families would be broadcast at once so our relatives would learn immediately of our safety.

# RED ✝ CROSS

MY FIRST CONTACT WITH THE INTERNATIONAL RED CROSS WAS AT DULAG LUFT, WERTZAL, GERMANY. THIS WAS AFTER A MONTH AND A HALF OF CAPTIVITY HAVING GONE ALL THIS TIME WITHOUT THE COMFORT THAT THESE ITEMS COULD AFFORD US. THE FOLLOWING ITEMS WERE GIVEN US.

| | |
|---|---|
| 1 SUIT CASE | 1 CAN TOOTH POWDER |
| 4 BARS TOILET SOAP | 1 SHOE BRUSH |
| 1 BANDAGE KIT | 1 CAN SHOE POLISH |
| 1 SEWING KIT | 1 HAIR BRUSH |
| 1 COMB | 2 BARS LAUNDRY SOAP |
| 2 PR. SHOE STRINGS | 1 CARTON GUM |
| 20 RAZOR BLADES | 3 HANDKERCHIEFS |
| 1 BOTTLE CASCARA TABLETS | 3 PR. SOCKS |
| 1 ROLL TOILET PAPER | 1 SUIT SUMMER UNDERWEAR |
| 1 PR. BEDROOM SLIPPERS | 2 SUITS WINTER UNDERWEAR |
| 1 KAKHI SHIRT | 1 WOOL CAP |
| 1 KAKHI TIE | 1 OVER COAT |
| 1 BOTTLE VITAMIN TABLETS | 1 SUIT FLANNEL PAJAMAS |
| 1 SHAVING SOAP | 2 BATH TOWELS |
| 1 SHAVING BRUSH | 5 PKS. CIGARETTES |
| 1 RAZOR | 1 JACKET (IF NEEDED) |
| 1 TOOTH BRUSH | 1 SWEATER (BRIDGE PORT, CONN.) |
| 1 TOOTH BRUSH CASE | 1 PIPE |
| | 2 PKGS. TOBACCO |

○────────○

AT STALAG LUFT I, BARTH, GERMANY, OUR PERMANENT CAMP, WE WERE GIVEN THESE ADDITIONAL ITEMS.

| | |
|---|---|
| 1 SUIT SUMMER UNDERWEAR | 1 WOOL O.D. SHIRT |
| 1 PR. WOOL O.D. PANTS | 2 PR. SOCKS |
| 1 BELT (IF NEEDED) | 1 SEWING KIT |
| 1 PR. SHOES (IF NEEDED) | |

At Wertzal after almost two months of starvation, no soap, hot water or showers and living in the same clothes 24 hours a day, this was what I received to make me feel like a human being again.

The guard left the room, and we all started writing glowing letters to alleviate the worry of our loved ones. Then it dawned on me that this was nothing but another trick to gain information and propaganda material. This was not the way to notify families of our well-being. That was the job of the International Red Cross. I got the attention of all the men in the room and told them to tear up their letters. They did so, and we walked out past the guard, who had a very surprised look on his face. This incident really was a small thing, but I felt that small things added up to big things, and I didn't want to give the Germans anything they could use.

On September 16 and 17, they took our Red Cross parcels and put them in a consolidated mess where we had three good meals a day. However, I was still sick and only nibbled at food for those two days. Fortunately, though, my burns had healed completely more than two weeks earlier, and I no longer had to deal with them.

On September 18, we boarded the train for the last time, headed for Barth, Germany, due north of Berlin on the Baltic Sea. We were each given a Red Cross food parcel to take on the train. I was still under the weather, and during the first two days ate only enough dried prunes from my package to keep up my strength. On the third morning I woke up ravenous and had a feast.

On September 22 our train pulled into the place that was to be my home until the Allies won a victory in Europe. We marched over to Stalag Luft I and I went through the gates. For the first time, I felt completely free to talk with my fellow officers and not worry about Germans hearing what I had to say. As I walked down between the buildings, old-timers leaned out of the windows looking for someone they recognized.

I heard a loud scream and John "Pappy" Medeiros jumped out of a window and came over to hug me. He was an old buddy from cadet flying school days. I had found a friend, someone I could trust, a place to call home and to be among friends again. It was a long journey from the beach head of Normandy, and what I had to face still wasn't a picnic, but it seemed a haven in a crazy world.

Indeed, my luck had begun to change. It turned out that Pappy was a "wheel" in the compound, which meant he had a job and a good one at that. He was in charge of handing out Red Cross food parcels and some of the Salvation Army gifts that arrived at the camp. He took me to his barracks, instead of the one to which I was to be assigned, and found a bed for me.

A portrait of me by N.J. Morrison.

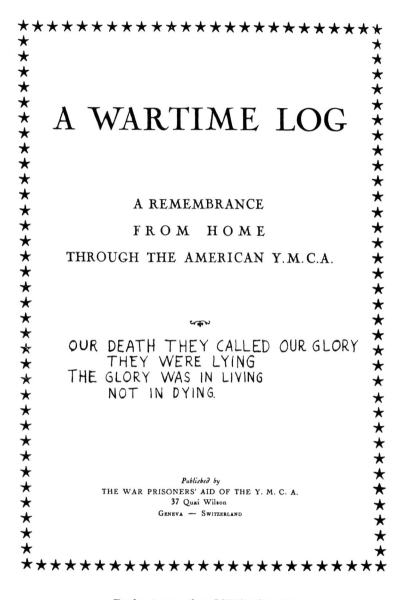

# A WARTIME LOG

## A REMEMBRANCE

## FROM HOME

## THROUGH THE AMERICAN Y.M.C.A.

OUR DEATH THEY CALLED OUR GLORY
THEY WERE LYING
THE GLORY WAS IN LIVING
NOT IN DYING.

Published by
THE WAR PRISONERS' AID OF THE Y. M. C. A.
37 Quai Wilson
GENEVA — SWITZERLAND

The front page of my POW Wartime Log.

# 14

## Stalag Luft I

After settling into my quarters, the most important thing to do next was to search the compound for fellow pilots and friends from the past. The first one I ran into was Lt. John E. Benbow from my outfit, who had been shot down August 15, just 16 days after my capture, and had been here at Stalag I for a couple of weeks. He brought me up to date on the squadron. The most interesting thing he had to tell me was that an hour after I was shot down, an order arrived sending me home for 30 days of R&R, or rest and recuperation. Including travel time, I would have been on my way back from California to my outfit at that time.

When I did return home after the war, a copy of this order was in my file. It was dated July 27. It had taken three days to get to me, a distance of no more than five to 10 miles − it had arrived just an hour too late to do me any good.

The prison camp was set up as if we were in England or the United States, with a chain of command in which the ranking American officers ran the camp. We all took orders as if we were back in the group flying. Colonel Henry R. Spicer was the commanding officer of our compound, one of many at Stalag I. The jobs to be done were divided up among the ranking officers and additional officers were assigned to carry out their orders. Colonel Spicer was the one who dealt with the German officer, Major Steinhauer, who was commander of our compound, and the two men treated each other with the respect due their ranks.

The barracks were wooden, prefabricated buildings placed on four-inch logs above the ground. The rooms were four small 8 x 16 ft. rooms and 10 large 16 x 24 ft. rooms. There was a central hallway running from end to end. I was in one of the large rooms, which was furnished with double wooden bunks with mattresses stuffed with excelsior wood shavings. There was also a large table with two benches and a small cast-iron wood stove for heating and cooking.

One of my first interests was to find out the chances for planning an escape, but I soon learned that there were to be no more attempted escapes from this camp. There was an escape committee that worked on plans and considered ideas of any of

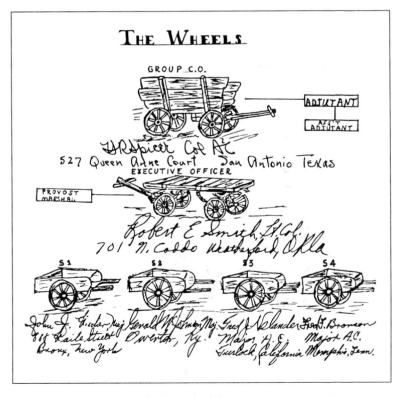

These were the big shot "wheels" running our compound.

the officers; however, the plans had all been put on hold because of the feeling that the war might be over by Christmas. The command did not want to risk the lives of the men at this stage of the game. Since we were at the most northern part of Germany on the Baltic Sea, it also was felt that even if there was a successful escape from the camp, the chances of getting out of Germany and back to England before the war was over were pretty slim.

But the escape committee remained very active making plans and looking for weaknesses in the German system. We didn't know what Hitler might do and we wanted to be in a position to get a few men out to get word back to the Allies or, in the event of a real catastrophe, to make a mass breakout.

Over the fence in the distance was another compound for Russian prisoners of war, who lived under completely different conditions from the Americans. From the beginning, the Germans

Behind the wire by Walt Rebello.

had not recognized the Geneva Convention when they rolled into Russia, and the Russians reciprocated.

The Russian prisoners drove the "honey bucket" wagon to clean the out-houses in our compound, and the Russians were a miserable sight to see.

This was my artist sketch
of what happened to thousands of us.

In the prison I was with Col. Henry Spicer, the commanding officer of our compound, along with his staff. I was really with the "wheels" now.

Walt Rebello shows what did not happen to me, MY SAD SAD STORY.
Twice I had passed up a chance of taking off July 26 and July 30.

My being on the Red Cross detail did not mean receiving extra food, as this was something none of us would have done even if we had a chance. But to have a job to keep busy was a godsend. In addition, there was something I received I might not have gotten if I had not been on this detail. Among the supplies that arrived from the YMCA were hard-cover books, "Wartime Logs," published by the YMCA's War Prisoners Aid in Geneva, Switzerland. I took one of these books and from that moment, I wrote a log beginning with my experiences from the time of my last mission until May 2, 1945, when we tore down the fences of the prison camp.

# 15

## Prison Camp—A New Life

Right after I arrived at the camp, I had started working with my roommate in the detail of handing out Red Cross food parcels. It was a great way to meet the other men in the camp. We distributed the parcels once a week, and it was something to look forward to. The parcels did not have the same contents every time, though one was as good as another and we did have variety.

For example, the number 10 parcel contained vitamin pills, Spam, sugar, canned roast or corned beef, raisins or prunes, coffee, crackers, two bars of soap, margarine, dates, five to nine packages of cigarettes, powdered milk, paté, jam or orange concentrate, sometimes peanut butter, salmon or tuna fish, cheese, two to four chocolate bars, which were the "D" bars carried by the troops in combat. This small box had to be nursed along for a week, giving us 1,000 calories a day. However, the 1,000 calories depended on us each receiving a parcel each week. We also received toilet paper as a supplement to what the Germans issued.

For some men, the cigarettes were the most important thing but for me, it was the chocolate bar that was packed with nutrition and satisfied my craving for sugar and chocolate the way the cigarettes satisfied the nicotine craving for the men who smoked.

I have never been able to verify who actually paid for the parcels but gathered that the British and American governments assembled the packages and delivered them to Red Cross units who brought them to Germany and our camps.

# NORTH No.2 COMPOUND

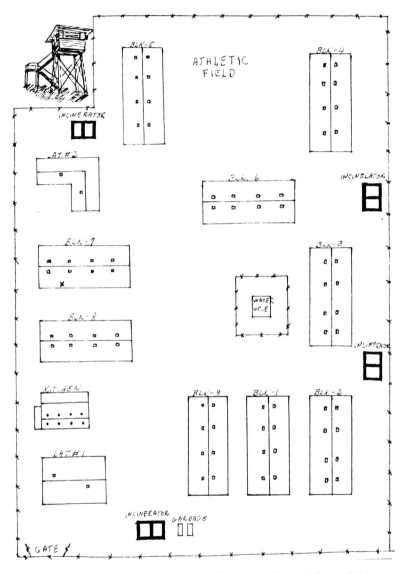

My first home, North No. 2 Compound, Block No. 6. It was in front of this building facing the athletic field that Col. Spicer gave his famous speech that landed him in solitary confinement until the end of the war.

Another important item in our diet was the German bread issued to us daily – it was like no bread we had ever seen or eaten. We called it black "broat." It was a heavy, moist, sour-tasting bread and the most unpalatable food one could imagine. If it dried out for a couple of weeks, it probably would have been more edible. There was a rumor that it was made of ersatz ingredients including sawdust. Since we couldn't keep it for two weeks, we toasted it to make it more bearable.

The bread was distributed by another detail of "Kriegies," the nickname for prisoners which was short for "kriegskafagnan," German for prisoner of war. I volunteered to slice the bread each morning in my room, since I had a steady hand and could slice it very thin. This made it easier to divide the bread evenly among us. We used the bread to stretch out our rations from morning 'til night.

I had heard that white bread was available for sick men, but I never confirmed that rumor. According to the Geneva Convention, the Germans were supposed to issue us each week a list of food including fresh meat, fat, potatoes, barley, and fresh vegetables. But all I remember receiving were cabbage and sauerkraut, $1^2/_3$ ounces flour, $3^1/_2$ ounces of wurst, cottage cheese, 5 ounces

This was the committee to distribute the Red Cross parcels. While writing this book in Dec. 1991 I took a close look and realized that I was the third man from the left.

of margarine, the black broat, ersatz jam, and salt.

Further, the food ration from the Germans was received on anything but a regular basis. I also remember receiving a small ration of Limburger cheese that was so strong-smelling and tasting that it was difficult to find anyone to take it. Once in a while, we also received horse meat, but very few men could stomach it. However, I found it very palatable, tasting a little bit on the sweet side. I got a double ration because of the aversion of the other prisoners. We had a feeling that the issuing of the horse meat coincided with raids by fighter planes in which horses were killed.

I had no way of knowing whether the Russian prisoners nearby were receiving food other than from the Germans – they were such a pathetic bunch of men that my heart went out to them.

Through a clandestine radio hidden in various places in the compounds, we were able to keep up with the progress of the war. The locations were tightly controlled by our own top officers, and only men needing to know where the radios were located were told of their locations. Men were assigned to listen to the BBC news each day, and the information was typed for us in our daily newspaper, Pow Wow. The newspaper was passed around to be

Having a hot shower every few months was a special occasion. We were marched out of the compound in groups of 40 for this very fast shower.

read in low tones in each room so that the "ferrets," Germans assigned to prevent escapes, could not know what was going on. We knew these men were constantly crawling around under our buildings and listening for any plans for escapes or other trouble-making.

From the BBC in London we heard about the Allied advances to new positions. One man also listened to the German radio and heard how the Allied lines were being held in certain locations. By plotting the movements, we could follow the retreat of the German "holding positions." As far as I knew, the radio was never found by the Germans.

I am still reminded of what life in prison camp was like when I look at my "Wartime Log," the scrapbook I covered with the little fabric that remained of my olive-drab wool jacket, which had been burned when I bailed out of my burning plane. In the log, which is still in good condition after nearly five decades, there are drawings, photos, written entries, and even samples of the ersatz food and other supplies we "Kriegies" received.

One page of the log I headed "Sad, Sad Stories," and the first person to sign it was my roommate, Pappy. His entry read: Capt. J.L. Medeiros, 1066 75th Ave., Oakland, Calif. Pilot —

This was the brot (bread) cart committee that
made the rounds every day.

129

P-51 – Show to Berlin. Hit by flak at 26,000 feet. Bailed out at 15,000 feet and landed in Meppen, Germany. POW.

As the months unfolded, the pages filled up with names and acts of heroism found in the pages of history.

Lt. C.C. Frascati, Pilot – B-24 – Lousy fighter cover. Bordeaux – never got there – Kaput by MEs.

THE WAY I GOT IT by Walt Rebello.
I learned 35 years later from my wingman
Lt. Woody Klinner Jr. how I was really shot down ...
(See Epilogue)

Lt. Jay E. Jones, Bombardier – B-17 – 190s rockets – no excuse, sir. Steyr, Austria.

Lt. James B. McArthur, Pilot – B-24 – Berlin – out of gas. Bailed out over Rotterdam.

2nd Lt. Coleman Jacobson, Bombardier –B-24 – Flak and fighters over Hanover.

Lt.Col. Francis E. Gabreski, Pilot – P-47 – Koblenz, 28 air victories.

And on and on the list of men filled the pages: Giltner, Rice, Meyers, Sherman, Solomon, O'Donnell, Eshleman, all heroes of the sky. I was determined that history be preserved in my Wartime Log.

Since ours was an officers' prisoner of war camp, it was unusual to find a sergeant, Walter E. Rebello, in the compound. He was a talented artist and did wonderful sketches for my "log."

One was a cartoon labeled "The Way I Got It." This told the story of how I was bombing a tank, blew up with one of our own bombs under me, and finally went down in flames.

Another POW that I had met on the first day in the camp was a Negro pilot officer, one of the very few in World War II. This was more than 45 years ago, and I don't remember now what we talked about, but I remember I wanted to know him. He seemed so alone, the only black with those thousands of white officers.

He had trained in an all-black unit in Alabama and then gone to Italy, where his unit had made an outstanding record. I never saw him again – he must have been moved to another compound.

After I settled down in the prison camp, I found my way to the library, and in my log I kept a record of the books I read. I also made comments, like "stinks" about "Under the Tonto Rim" by Zane Grey. Another book, "The Gossip: The Life and Times of Walter Winchell" by McKelway, I rated "poor."

Among the books I enjoyed were "How Green Was My Valley" by Richard Llewelyn, "The Man in the Iron Mask" by Alexander Dumas, "Lost Horizon" by James Hilton, and "Rebecca" by Du Maurier. The one I remember best to this day was not a novel but "Essentials of Business Law" by Edward M. Kanzer. That was one of the few items I carried home with me at the end of the war.

I spent many hours walking around the compound within the fenced-in area. This was one of the few activities that was enjoyed by everyone. We walked in groups or sometimes with one companion, or alone.

The powdered milk called "Klim" (milk spelled backwards) was our staff of life. By Don Ross.

This was a way to satisfy the need for privacy. Walking alone undisturbed with one's mind wandering was like being out in an open meadow with nothing but the sound of the wind. It was not only healthful, but also served as an outlet during the long uneventful days. It was pleasant during the nice fall weather but when the cold winter winds swept down from the north over the Baltic Sea, we did little walking. I don't remember much snow in our area, but the cold wet rain went right through to our bones. I spent many days in bed with my clothes on underneath a blanket and with more clothes piled on top. The only things sticking out were my head and one hand holding my book.

Because of the YMCA and their gathering together of the outpouring of contributions from the American people, we had

# FOOD! FOOD!! FOOD!!!

## SUNDAY

| BREAKFEAST | LUNCH | SUPPER |
|---|---|---|
| BARLEY | FRIED POTATOES | CREAMED POTATOES W/CHEESE |
| PRUNES | CREAMED CORN BEEF | FRIED SPAM W/RAISINS |
| | TOAST | BOILED CABBAGE |
| | | PLAIN CAKE W/CHOC ICING |

BARLEY IS ISSUED OUT ONCE OR TWICE A WEEK. IF WE GET ENOUGH THERE IS SOMETIMES ENOUGH TO HAVE FOR THE NEXT DAY AS IN THIS CASE.

## MONDAY

| BREAKFEAST | LUNCH | SUPPER |
|---|---|---|
| BARLEY (LEFT OVER) | FRIED POTATOES | ROAST BEEF (RARE) |
| TOAST + PEANUT BUTTER | CREAMED SPAM | BOILED POTATOES |
| | TOAST | RAW CABBAGE |
| | | TOAST |

ROAST BEEF IS A RARITY AND WE HAVE IT ONCE EVERY OTHER WEEK APPROX. THE GERMAN BARLEY HAS A BAD REPUTATION FOR HAVING WORMS AND BLACK SPECKS SHOW THE PREVIOUS PRESENCE OF RATS. WHO ARE WE KRIEGIES TO BE PARTICULAR.

## TUESDAY

| BREAKFEAST | LUNCH | SUPPER |
|---|---|---|
| TOAST + GERMAN CHEESE | CHEESE ON TOAST | CORN BEEF HASH |
| PRUNES | PATÉ ON TOAST | TOAST |
| | | RAW CABBAGE |

WE ARE CUTTING DOWN ON OUR CONSUMPTION OF R.C. CHEESE FOR LEAN DAYS. IF MORE PKGS. DON'T COME IN WE WILL RECEIVE ONE R.C. BOX EVERY 14 DAY.

A menu for the week. This food was received in the Red Cross parcels. During some periods we received very few parcels.

things that made it possible to make long boring hours into days of activity.

Musical instruments of all kinds not only meant that we had a band, but also provided a chance for some "Kriegies" to learn to play. The library had books for pleasure reading and also school books to study, "how to" books for crafts, and religious books.

Many of the volumes came from the British Red Cross and the Order of St. John.

We had all kinds of athletic equipment, including clothes for sports. We played football, baseball, volleyball, and had great boxing matches.

There were art supplies for all kinds of craft classes, office and school supplies, Christmas decorations for the holidays, a phonograph and popular and classical records. My leisure time was spent playing baseball, touch football, devouring books, and listening to the records. I got a great deal of pleasure out of the group activities.

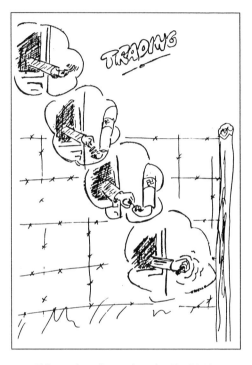

When we had plenty of Red Cross parcels, some of the men would make a delicious brew from the prunes, raisins, and sugar – it was a pretty potent drink.

This was how it was done for the POWs authorized to trade with the Germans.

In October, my starvation diet of August and September apparently caught up with me. I suffered with boils over my body and even next to my mouth. I was unable to eat and the boils became so severe that I had to be hospitalized. The doctor said they had a new medication from England that was supposed to kill infection. It was called penicillin, developed the previous year by Alexander Fleming, a bacteriologist. They had a very small amount of this serum, enough for only one shot, which the doctor gave me. It worked like a miracle and in a few days, I was on the mend and back in my barracks, ravenous to catch up on all the food I had passed up.

Quite a bit of trading went on between the Kriegies and the Germans. We weren't supposed to trade with them, but some of the fellows did it anyway. A few had authorization, especially those who spoke German, were allowed to trade food, cigarettes and soap for things they wanted from the outside.

Since being captured, I had learned that Goering, the head of the German Luftwaffe, not only kept a tight rein over his own air force but also over officers from the Allied air forces that had been taken prisoner of war. Many times the S. S. Black Shirts and Gestapo under Heinrich Himmler had been rebuffed and stopped when they tried to punish airmen for wrong doing. We were Goering's babies.

This was great to watch boxing matches but
no one wanted to box when we were short on rations.

The wash room.
Here we also took our sponge bath in the bitter cold weather.

A "Kriegie" cooking dinner.

# 16

## Colonel Spicer's Fateful Talk

Col. Henry Spicer was the commanding officer of our Compound No. 2. I was in block 6 with him, and we often played cards together. With his corn cob pipe in his mouth and a big fancy handlebar mustache, he was the picture of authority. A very dynamic leader, he had been commanding officer of the 357th Fighter Group and was brought down on a sweep of the Cherbourg Peninsula in his P-51 Mustang, "Tony Boy." (The plane was named for his young son, whom I wrote to more than 40 years later.) Colonel Spicer's plane had been hit in the coolant by light flak and crashed into the English Channel. He spent two days in the water and was in bad condition and unable to walk when he was finally picked up by the Germans.

On November 1, 1944, we were roused out in the morning for "appell" (roll call), and we lined up in the middle of the field. Colonel Spicer called us to attention and then turned the command over to Major Steinhauer, the German commandant, for the counting of the prisoners. The German guards counted all the men and reported the full count to the major. The numbers were correct, and the German major turned the prisoners back to Colonel Spicer for dismissal. But before dismissing us, he ordered the men to assemble in front of block 6 and gave this talk:

"Lads, as you can see, this isn't going to be any fireside chat. Someone has taken the steel bar off the south latrine door. The Germans want this bar back. They have tried to find it, and I've tried to find it. We have had no success. The Germans have threatened to cut off our coal ration if this bar isn't found by 12 noon. I don't know if this is a threat or not, but we must return this bar to the Germans. Anyone having information, report to my room after this talk. There will be no disciplinary action taken against anyone.

"Yesterday an officer (Major Benson) was put in the cooler for two weeks. He had two counts against him. The first was failure to obey the order of a German officer. That is beside the point. The second was failure to salute a German officer of lower rank."

"The Articles of the Geneva Convention say to salute all officers of equal or higher rank. The Germans in this camp have put out an order that we must salute all German officers, whether lower or higher rank. My order to you is salute all German officers of equal or higher rank."

"I have noticed that many of you are becoming too buddy-buddy with the Germans. Remember that we are still at war with the Germans. They are still our enemies and are doing everything they can to win this war. Don't let him fool you around this camp because he is a dirty lying sneak and can't be trusted."

"As an example of the type of enemy you have to deal with, the British were forced to retreat in the Arnheim area. They had to leave the wounded in the hospital. The Germans took the hospital and machine-gunned all those British in their beds."

"In Holland behind the German lines, a woman with a baby in her arms was walking along the road evacuating the battle zone. Some British prisoners were passing her. She gave them the V for victory sign. A German soldier saw her and without hesitation swung his gun around and shot her on the spot."

"They are a bunch of murderous no-good liars and if we have to stay here for 15 years to see all the Germans killed, then it will be worth it."

At this point, there were loud cheers from all the men. The colonel then turned to the German major and non-coms standing at the side.

"For your information, these are my own personal opinions, and I'm not attempting to incite riot or rebellion. They are my opinions and not necessarily the opinions of my men."

Again there were more loud cheers.

Then the colonel faced the men again and said, "That is all, men, and remember what I have told you."

Within several hours, the colonel was in solitary confinement and Lt.Col. Wilson, second in command, had been threatened with solitary confinement the next day if the iron bar did not show up.

(Colonel Spicer remained in solitary and was not released until April 30, 1945, when the Americans took over the camp.)

After he was taken to solitary, we were told to keep anything from the Germans that could be used against the men or Colonel Spicer in case of a court-martial for incitement of a riot or rebellion.

I had realized that Colonel Spicer had made a momentous speech that should not be lost. As soon as I returned to my room, I gathered my roommates around to help me write down his speech word for word. As we reconstructed the sentences, I wrote them down in a small 6 by 6-inch scratch pad which I then copied into my log book. The original notes are still folded in my log.

Meanwhile, the same day, the steel bar showed up, and we did not lose our coal ration.

I had hidden my log in a secret place between my bunk and the wall, not wanting the Germans to find it in their searches. With a knife, I cut out of my log the 10 pages of names and addresses of my fellow pilots that showed the types of planes they had flown and where and how they were shot down. I put this, along with a copy of the colonel's speech, in a sealed can and buried it under the barracks. It wasn't until January that I dug up the can when I moved to another compound.

Colonel Spicer was court-martialed and sentenced to death, to take effect in three months. This would have been on April

1, 1945, but by that time the war was going so badly for Germany that the sentence was not carried out. His story was told in the newspapers after 6,000 of us American pilots were released from the prisoner-of-war camp near Barth.

In my log there is a cartoon by one of the men, Don Ross, who was an artist, that had been sketched one week before Colonel Spicer gave his fateful speech to the "Kriegies." The sketch shows us playing a hot game of Parcheesi with me facing the artist. Colonel Spicer was shown from the back with this big handlebar mustache sticking out and two majors of his staff on each side.

The Allied commanders in the various Stalag Luft camps had different theories on how to deal with the Germans. Some of them were of the opinion that the more we cooperated with them, the easier it would be on us.

# PW Doomed For Pep Talk

Col. Henry R. Spicer, of San Antonio, Texas, former Eighth AF fighter group commander, was sentenced to death by the Germans for giving a pep talk to Americans in a PW camp.

The airman was saved from a firing squad by the arrival of Russian troops who overran Stalagluft One, near Barth, Germany. His story was told after more than 9,000 Allied prisoners, most of them American airmen, had been evacuated from Barth in three days by Eighth AF Fortresses.

Before his rescue, Spicer was kept in solitary confinement in a tiny cell for six months, while other American officers in the camp sought to have the death sentence lifted.

Spicer was captured after parachuting into the English Channel on May 3, 1944. He was sentenced to death several months later.

All I did was explain to the men that things were pretty bad to keep up their morale," the colonel declared, describing his pep talk.

This was a good caricature of Col. Henry R. Spicer who stood up to the Germans and put a stronger backbone in every POW.

A hot game of parchesi. Col. Spicer's back faces me
with one Major on each side. Sketch by Don Ross.

At Stalag Luft I, Colonel Spicer had a different policy. His philosophy, as I saw it, was to cause as much trouble and play as many tricks as we could get by with in order to harass the Germans. We paid for this by having more "appell" turn-outs in the middle of the day when we would have to stand at attention for an hour or more. The "goons" (German officers or soldiers) and the "ferrets" would go through our rooms looking for anything that was illegal for us to have. We felt this was a small price to pay. Colonel Spicer was a good example of a commander who challenged the Germans every chance he got.

In my block, I met another top ace, Lt. Col. Francis S. Gabreski, who had flown a P-47 and had 28 air victories to his credit. Returning from one mission, he approached a German airdrome where there were fighter planes. Since he had ammunition left, Gabreski dove down and strafed the airdrome. This type of action taken after a bomber escort mission had not been condoned by the high brass at first, but after Gabreski and others showed that it was a way to do more damage to the Germans on

Life Magazine Oct. 11, 1948.
Bomber pilot Jimmy Stewart honors 8 of the 38
Congressional Medal of Honor heroes.  Lt. Red Morgan third from left.

Kriegie Red Morgan on the hot water committee.  He was awarded
the Congressional Medal of Honor for valor on a B-17 bombing mission.

the ground, the senior officers saw the wisdom of the approach.

On the day that Gabreski dropped down from a high altitude to fly across the German air field, he began strafing planes that seemed to have been lined up for him. Just as he was about to pull up, he saw one more plane ahead. He lowered the nose a little to get a final shot, and his prop touched the ground, but he managed to fly some distance before he bellied in. Eventually, he was captured by the Germans and was taken before Hanns Scharff at Dulag Luft.

However, most of the POWS in our camp were shot down in B-17s and B-24s. In the air war over Europe, the bombers were taking the brunt of the battle. Often anywhere from 5 to 20 bombers were shot down on one mission, each plane carrying a full crew. The loss of men, like me, flying fighter planes on the same mission was a fraction of the loss of the bombers. Meanwhile, the fighter pilot's war, as illustrated in Gabreski's case, had changed. They were now hitting marshalling yards and airfields, surprising German positions on the ground.

Another top ace said in a story he wrote, "Coming down and facing the anti-aircraft fire and machine guns on the ground was even tougher than fighting the German planes in the sky." As time went on, more and more fighter aces were lost, not due to aerial combat, but by being shot down by ground fire.

In a note of humor appreciated by the airmen who had been taken prisoner, a notice was posted on our camp bulletin board on November 19, 1944. It read:

"If you pilots can hit spot landings time after time,
And you navigators can hit a point 3,000 miles away,
And you bombardiers can hit a pickle barrel from 20,000 feet.
Why can't you gentlemen hit the hole in the toilet seat.
Keep your eyes off the balls and on the hole!"
By order of Lieutenant Colonel Wilson.

On November 24, we got bad news. We experienced our first shortage of Red Cross parcels, which meant a cut in rations of 50 percent with two men sharing each parcel. The following week, the same thing happened.

With the cold weather and Christmas coming, this was the last thing we had expected, but we just drew in our belts and waited to see what would happen.

# 17

## Xmas–Kriegie Style

On December 8 we received our full ration of food parcels, and we "Kriegies" on this detail who saw the full load arrive, spread the joy through the compound.

It was at about this time that the Germans gave us orders to open our Red Cross packages before handing them out. We had to puncture the cans of food in order to eliminate any chance of hoarding food for planned escapes or a massive breakout. However, we made such a big fuss that the order was soon rescinded.

During the last two months we had been kept in a high pitch of anticipation, reading the Pow Wow and making bets on when the war would end. The Allied advances had slowed down, not only because of a severe winter but also because the German soldiers were fighting ferociously in their homeland. In addition, Hitler was giving orders for no retreats at any cost; the number of German soldiers killed apparently did not bother him.

Most of us had given up hope of a victory before Christmas, but two men made an unusual bet that the war would end by the holiday. We would have to wait until Christmas day to see who won and what the bet was.

We didn't know what the Germans would do as the Russians advanced from the east, and we didn't know what Hitler would do to us. Many of us decided to prepare. The first thing I did was draw a map, which I thought was so good that even MacMillan would approve. I detailed roads in red, rivers in blue, woods in green, and the main railroads in black, just as in a professional map. I still have the map because I folded it up and put it in my Wartime Log.

In mid-December we got a new commanding officer, Col. Hubert "Hub" Zemke. He had led the 56th Fighter Group flying P-47s, and under his command the group had the top score of 525 planes shot down. The P-47 had demonstrated its ability to fly against the best German fighters as well as against ground forces. Gabby Gabreski had been one of Zemke's men in the 56th group.

As a fighter pilot and knowledgeable man, Colonel Zemke had been sent on a mission to Russia in 1941. His job was to supervise the training of Russian pilots flying P-40 Tomahawks that were being shipped from America. We thought that if it were the Russians who liberated us from the Germans, he would be the ideal officer to deal with them.

On his last combat mission, Zemke had bailed out of a P-51 Mustang over Germany during a violent thunderstorm. The storm had started literally tearing his plane to pieces when he was thrown out of his seat. Before he arrived at Stalag Luft I, he had spent a month and a half in a hospital and at the interrogation center with Hanns Scharff.

On December 22 we received a happy surprise – the Red Cross had sent special Christmas parcels in addition to the regular food rations. While there were not enough for all, we did receive four parcels to share among five men. However, when we were halfway through issuing the parcels, a new contingent of POWs arrived and we had to re-allot the parcels in order to share equally with them. The Christmas packages each contained a photograph and a painting. The ones I received seemed especially appropriate – one showed cotton pickers in my home state of Arkansas and the other was a copy of a painting of San Francisco in the 1840s where my wife's family lived and where I would live in the future. There was also Prince Albert tobacco, three packages of cigarettes, a wash cloth, deck of cards, canned plum pudding, boned turkey, honey, butter, jam, nuts, candy, bouillon cubes, deviled ham, Vienna sausages, fruit bars, American cheese, and cherries.

We now had a couple of days to prepare for our Christmas dinner, print up the menu and decide how to prepare the food.

We awoke Christmas morning for "appell" on a bitter cold day. After counting the "Kriegies," Major Steinhauer turned us over for dismissal. It was then we witnessed the payment of the debt by the man who had wagered the war would be over by Christmas. In September 1944, Stark had said to Johnson, "I'll kiss your ass if the war isn't over by Christmas." Stepping out before 1,500 "Kriegies," Second Lt. Stanley M. Johnson of Port Allegany, Penn., lowered his pants and leaned over. Second Lt. Richard D. Stark of Tampa, Fla., came forward with a bucket of hot water and a towel. After washing Johnson's rear end, he folded the towel, placed it over the crack and gave the "cheek" a good kiss.

Fifteen hundred men let out with a cheering and clapping that could be heard in all the other compounds. The German Major Steinhauer stood there with his guards, shaking his head in amazement, not believing what he had witnessed. We were then dismissed.

There was a mail call before our Christmas dinner. I had stood in line at Stalag I for three months without receiving a single letter. One of the most difficult experiences in prison had not been the lack of food or fear for my life, but worry about what my wife and mother were going through, not knowing whether I was alive or dead. This time I heard my name called and couldn't believe it – I had received my first letter in prison from my wife – and they knew I was alive. This was the best of all days. Furthermore, I realized that this was not her first letter to me since she had numbered it and that there would be more to come.

Later, 10 of us sat down for a sumptuous Christmas repast. They were Lt. James B. "Flat Top" McArthur, Lt. B. M. "Nix"

Eshleman, Lt. Walter E. "Bootie" Payne, Lt. Arthur B. "Creamed Beef" Meyers, Lt. Eric H. "Baldy" Sherman, Lt. Jake "Chihuahua" Feagles, and Lt.C. F. "Scotty" Frascati. We were all thankful that

In November 1944 there were all kinds of bets on
the end of the war by Xmas. This was the craziest bet of them all.

we had been able to surmount the odds and could sit here looking forward to a future of happiness with our families.

A few days later a "Kriegie" bet me a D bar that I wouldn't get another letter from home before March 1. Being an optimist, I took him up on the bet. In February, I received my second letter, and he paid off with half a chocolate bar. Because of the shortage of food parcels, I didn't have the heart to make him pay a full bar. In prison everyone took his debts very seriously.

A few days later after Christmas, we were notified that all of the Jewish POWS in the entire camp would be moved out of their barracks and consolidated in one compound. On January 10 I left my friends behind and moved out of North No. 2 Compound to No. 1 Compound, where I met new "Kriegies," all Jewish. The Germans had told us that Hitler had given the order that we were going to be annihilated. My attitude about danger had always been to ignore what I couldn't control, and

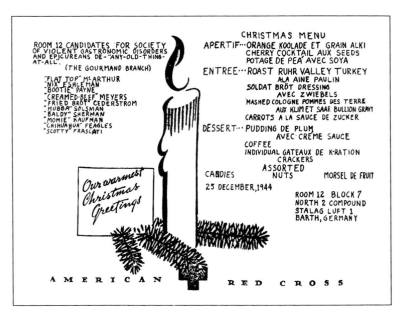

A special Xmas day menu written by me for an elite society of epicureans.

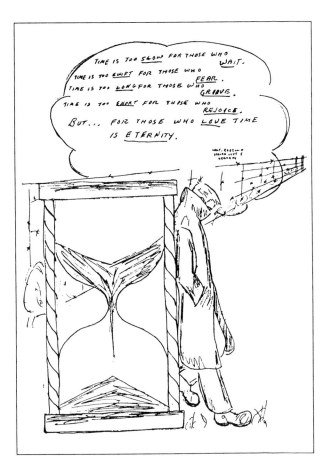

Walt Rebello paraphrased a famous poem with a sketch of a sad POW.

I hadn't given a damn about their threats before. I had always been a fatalist, and believed my death was ordained a long time ago. There was nothing I could do about it. None of the other men in the barracks carried on or seemed worried, either. They seemed to feel the same way I did.

Of course, history later told us of Hitler's grand plan – the annihilation of all Jews in Europe. Our fate was only a small step for him.

The last thing I did as I left my old barracks was to dig up my tin can from under the building. These were the papers I was able to put back into my Wartime Log.

Meanwhile, the prison life was becoming grimmer in other

# To all Prisoners of War!

## The escape from prison camps is no longer a sport!

Germany has always kept to the Hague Convention and only punished recaptured prisoners of war with minor disciplinary punishment.

Germany will still maintain those principles of international law.

But England has besides fighting at the front in an honest manner instituted an illegal warfare in non combat zones in the form of gangster commandos, terror bandits and sabotage troops even up to the frontiers of Germany

They say in a captured secret and confidential English military pamphlet

## THE HANDBOOK
## OF MODERN IRREGULAR WARFARE:

"... the days when we could practice the rules of sportsmanship are over. For the time being every soldier must be a potential gangster and must be prepared to adopt their methods whenever necessary

"The sphere of operations should always include the enemy's own country, any occupied territory, and in certain circumstances such neutral countries as he is using as a source of supply."

England has with these instructions opened up a non military form of gangster war!

Germany is determined to safeguard her homeland and especially her war industry and provisional centres for the fighting fronts. Therefore it has become necessary to create strictly forbidden zones, called death zones, in which all unauthorized trespassers will be immediately shot on sight.

Escaping prisoners of war, entering such death zones, will certainly lose their lives. They are therefore in constant danger of being mistaken for enemy agents or sabotage groups.

Urgent warning is given against making future escapes!

In plain English: Stay in camp where you will be safe! Breaking out of it is now a damned dangerous act.

The chances of preserving your life are almost nil!

All police and military guards have been given the most strict orders to shoot on sight all suspected persons.

## Escaping from prison camps has ceased to be a sport!

In March 1945 the Germans were finding
excuses for ignoring the rules of the Geneva Convention.

ways. On January 5, the Germans posted a new regulation: "It is strictly forbidden to trespass upon the area between the warning wire and the barbed-wire fence. The same applies to touching the warning wire." The guards were given new orders to fire without warning, as had been the custom before. Until then, we had used the warning wire, a single strand two feet high, on which to hang our laundry and air our blankets.

These new regulations were not in accordance with the Geneva Convention.

At the camp, when an alarm was sounded, we prisoners had to report back to our rooms and remain there until the alert was over. Doors, windows, and shutters were to be closed during the alarms.

One afternoon about a month after the new rules were issued, a "Kriegie" was asleep on his bunk and when he awakened, he did not realize there was an alert under way. He opened the door and stepped out, but when he saw the grounds were deserted, he quickly turned around to get back in. He was not quick enough, however; the guards in the tower fired upon him and he fell forward through the open door, dead.

A few weeks later a similar incident happened to another prisoner. This time, after waking up, he opened a window and shutters and jumped out. Before he could jump back in, he was killed. In both cases there was not even a remote possibility that the men were trying to escape.

Meanwhile, in my new quarters with five other men, I began developing new interests. I no longer had the Red Cross parcel detail; so I started a new life of friends and activity.

The first thing I did was to become a "tin smith." I began saving the largest of the empty cans, and I was able to get a hammer and a pair of scissors. First I opened and flattened the cans and then I found that by folding the tin like paper, I was able to put pieces together and make larger sheets of any size I wanted. I made several sizes of shallow baking pans for cakes and deep ones for cooking the main dishes on the stove. An extra set of dishes for the meal came in handy, too. We had a small iron stove, not only to heat our room, but also for all of our cooking. I made a blower to keep the fire going. Other items I made included a grater, potato masher, and rolling pin. I also made items for my new friends in the other rooms. I must say I was one hell of a worker who made a lot of noise, hammering away on a bench.

Other "Kriegies" made various articles. One saved tin foil from cigarette packages and cans containing lead. He melted these down to use for molding decorative articles like Allied and German insignia. He sold them to people, often for packs of cigarettes, which were like money, to buy knicknacks. I still have four lead

```
Kriegsgefangenenlager No. 1 der Lw.          Barth, 5.1.1945
   - Gruppe I c Lagerführung -

To:  The Senior American Officer and Senior Compound Officers

          Re:  Camp Order No. 1

1.  It is strictly forbidden to trespass upon the area between
    warning wire and barbed-wire fence. The same applies to touching
    the warning wire. The guards received instruction to make
    immediate use of their fire-arms and to shoot, without any
    previous challenge, at every P.o.w. who touches the warning wire.
    Balls that were thrown into the area between warning wire and
    barbed-wire fence while playing, may be fetched out once a day
    in the presence of a guard. It is also prohibited to hang laundry
    blankets etc. over warning wire or to leave same in the open air
    over night.

2.  When air alarm is sounded, all Ps.o.w. are to immediately proceed
    to their blocks or they are expected to remain in the rooms in
    which they are at the moment when alert is given. Doors and windows
    must be closed by the Ps.o.W. themselves. Ps.o.W. who are on the
    way outside the compound when alarm is given, will be directly
    taken back to their compound by the guard who accompanies them.
    The guards received instruction to fire, without previous challenge,
    at ps.o.w. who appear at the window during an air alarm. When a
    preliminary warning /öffentliche Luftwarnung/ is sounded after
    dusk, the Ps.o.w. are to behave as if it were
    alarm. In addition they are to see to it that windows and doors
    are well blacked out. The Block Commanders are made responsible
    that these regulations are strictly carried out by the Ps.o.W.
    of the individual blocks.

3.  Furthermore attention is drawn to the fact that there must be ut-
    most cleanliness inside and outside the living quarters as well
    as on the whole camp area. The Senior Compound Officers are made
    responsible for same.

4.  w.e.f. Monday, January 8th 1945 lights will be switched off at
    2200 hours. Therefore special permissions /Glee Club, working
    party for the theatre/ can no longer be granted till later than
    2130 hours.

                              gez. Jäger.
                    Oberst u. Gruppenleiter.
```

In January 1945 the Germans started getting meaner.
Some of our men were killed for no real reason.

Milton Plattner 2ⁿᵈ Lt.  B-17    INNSBRUCK - TARGET
542 Van Siclen Ave.      N     NEW ME-410 PLANT AT AUGSBURG
Brooklyn, N.Y.                 SHOT DOWN BY ME-110s
                (PLAT)         DATE - 12/19/43 - PARACHUTED FROM
                               22,000 FT. LANDED ON ONE OF ALPS
Charles K. Hecht Jr.  P.47     MTS.
1202 Cedar Ave.                LITTLE "B" ESCORT NOV. 29, 43.
Columbus, Ga.          P       3 OR 4 FIGHTS, BUT NOT SHOT
                               DOWN. RAN OUT OF GAS.
                               SYMPATHY WANTED AAHHHH. T.S.
              (CHARLIE)        CRASH LANDED IN HOLLAND.

Arthur "RED" Carmell   B17     SHOT DOWN IN NORWAY BY A
33 Wales St.           B.      WOMAN FLACK GUNNER. I KNEW
Boston, Mass.                  ONE WOULD GET ME SOONER OR
                               LATER. NOV 16, 1943
              (RED)

Leo B. Margolis        CAPT.   DUMB BOMBING MARBLE
427 Washington St.     P-40    ARCH AIRDROME, LIBYA
Brookline, Mass.       P       AFRICA. (DEC. 10, 1942). OUR
                               BOOSTING WHILE COMBATING
                               ME 109s CAUSED ENGINE TO
                               DISINTEGRATE. CRASH LANDED IN
              (MARGO)          DESERT. -

Milton J. Kaplan       2ⁿᵈ Lt. The unusual occurred - engine trouble.
10 Fessenden St.       B-17    Bailed out at Haywdo. Crashed Holland, returning
Mattapan, Mass.        N       from Brunswick - Jan. 30, 1944.
                               Recommended reading - "The Horror Story of
              (KAP)            Lt. M.J. Kaplan" - McKellan Publisher.

Albert J. Ricci
2ⁿᵈ Lt. G.C.
30 High St.,
Keene New Hamp.
MARTIN FEINGOLD 2nd.   B-17    Shot down on Münster raid by fighters
c/o B. HABERMAN               March 23 d. 1944
119-13 Liberty Ave.
RICHMOND HILL, LONG ISLAND  NAV.
N.Y.
              (MORTY)

In my new compound I added my new Jewish roommates.
Note: Capt. Leo Margolis had been shot down in Libya, Dec. 10, 1942.

154

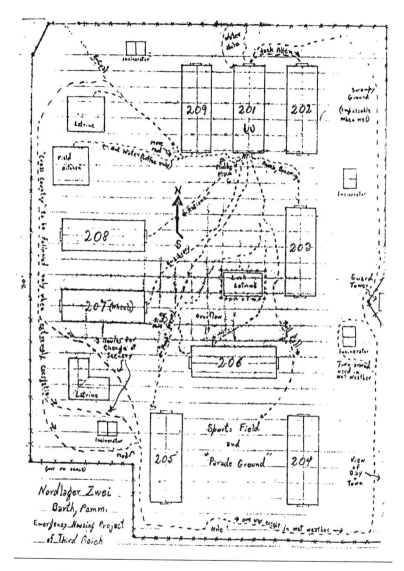

This was Compound #1 that I was transferred to in January 1945 in preparation for the annihilation of all the Jewish fighters in the camp.

insignia in my wartime memorabilia.

Cooking had always been one of my greatest pleasures in camp, but it began to mean even more in this barracks where I lived with a smaller number of people. We spent time each week writing out menus, trying to concoct a balanced diet with what we had available, assigning jobs for each man to do. All of this took a good portion of the day and was pleasant.

Here is a recipe for chocolate cake that took half a day to concoct and bake: Two quarts of boiling water – stir in 10 ground crackers crushed with my tin rolling pin. Add four heaping table-spoons of Klim (powdered milk) and $1/2$ cup sugar. The chocolate flavoring came from scraped D bars. Then it was made into a paste and cooked until done. For the topping, mix two tablespoons sugar, one heaping spoon of butter. Mix thoroughly with a little water and pour over the chocolate pudding. Wow! This was really special.

We also made a pretty tasty mayonnaise by mixing our powdered milk with water and adding the oil from cans of sardines.

My favorite, though, was the large pan of chocolate cake made from the D bars.

For the POW who wanted to keep busy, there was plenty to do. For example, January 13, 1945 was a day of typical com-pound activities. There were Catholic and Protestant services in the morning. There were classical concerts in the afternoon, and many classes we could take, including American government, drama, ping pong, German and Spanish, American history, public speaking, art, and accounting, which was one of my favorites.

However, beginning in January we started living on a star-vation diet. Instead of one parcel weekly, we were cut in half for the entire month.

Although the winter of 1944 - 45 had little snow, the cold, wet winds sweeping out of the north over the Baltic Sea made life unbearable outside. The Germans also were cutting our rations of coal. With less food and coal and the bitter weather, we were miserable. We felt the end of the war was close but the rainbow was still out of reach.

There were card games going on constantly in the barracks. I enjoyed watching the poker games, but I was not a gambler myself. I played hearts, pinochle, Parcheesi, and my favorite game, bridge. The poker players preferred playing for money, and payment could be promises to pay, cigarettes, or anything else they could use to bargain with.

A lot of time in camp was spent talking about food because we were always hungry. Now that I was with the Jewish men, I began to hear a new menu discussed. In Vicksburg I had not been exposed to the wonderful ethnic Jewish food that one found in New York. There were coffee cakes and sponge cakes, humentachen (a holiday treat), honey cake, and honey balls. Some of the foods I had never heard of: lox and cream cheese on bagels, marinated herring, pickled onions, pickled tomatoes, lauchen kugel, matzo ball soup. Fried matzo seemed to be a favorite around Passover time. This was matzos soaked in milk and eggs and fried in butter. Gedempte was a roast brisket and potato dish. There was also sweet and sour tongue, lox soaked overnight and fried with scrambled eggs and onions and served with toasted bagels. Knishes were pastries stuffed with meat and

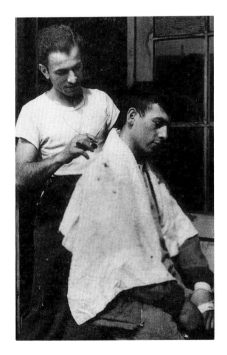

This barber isn't me but I did this for many of my fellow "Kriegies."

potatoes, and blintzes were crepes filled with cottage cheese and served with sour cream and jam. They also talked about strudel (a pastry), tzimas (a carrot dish) served with meat, and potatoes and two other things I had not heard of – kishka, which was stuffed intestines, and heltzel, which was stuffed chicken necks.

For months these foods were talked about by the hour. I learned a lot about ethnic food, but mostly we talked about home-cooked dishes. These memories brought us closer to our loved ones at home.

Throughout our imprisonment, we kept up the chores no matter what the conditions were. We had to wash our clothes regularly as well as our blankets. Our mattresses, sacks filled with packing material wood shavings, were aired out. Under the conditions we lived, it was vital to our health to keep everything clean.

DEAR
I AM GOING TO SUE FOR A DIVORCE. MOTHER AND I HAVE TALKED IT OVER AND SINCE YOU HAVE BEEN GONE SO LONG (4 YEARS) WE DECIDED IT WAS BEST
BRITISH W/O FROM WIFE

SON
WE ARE NOT SENDING YOU ANY PARCELS. WE HEAR YOU CAN BUY ALL YOU NEED IN THE STORES NEAR YOUR CAMP
LT. L.B. FROM HOME

DEAR JOHN
I GAVE YOUR GOLF CLUBS TO A GERMAN COLONEL
POW HERE IN CANADA. I HOPE YOU DONT MIND!
(JOHN WROTE BACK AND TOLD HER TO GET HIS GOLF CLUBS BACK. HIS COUNTRY CLUB IM-MEDIATELY CANCELLED HIS MEMBERSHIP FOR NOT BEING A GENTLEMAN.

A PRISONER OF WAR RECEIVED A SWEATER FROM A WOMAN THROUGH THE RED CROSS; AND UPON RECEIVING IT WROTE A LETTER OF THANKS. SHE WROTE BACK. — "I'm SORRY TO HEAR THAT A PRISONER RECEIVED THE SWEATER I KNITTED. I MADE IT FOR A FIGHTING MAN

158

DEAR ———
    I AM INCLOSING A CALENDAR. THOUGHT
IT MIGHT COME IN HANDY AS IT HAS
SEVERAL YEARS ON IT.
                        LT. L.B.S. FROM AUNT


A PILOT HITS GERMAN SOIL AND SAYS "WELL I MAY
HAVE PLENY OF TROUBLE AHEAD BUT AT LEAST
THE WORRIES OF HOME ARE OVER FOR THE DURATION."


THE FOLLOWING LETTERS WERE RECEIVED BY POW'S IN
THIS CAMP.

MY DARLING HUSBAND,
     DO YOU GET TO TOWN VERY OFTEN WHILE A
POW
                        LT. M.C.L. FROM WIFE

DEAR:
     IT MUST BE NICE TO BE ABLE TO PLAY GOLF AGAIN
                    CAPT. S.W.C. FROM WIFE

DEAR
     PLEASE HAVE A PICTURE TAKEN & SEND IT TO ME
                        LT. J.C.E. FROM WIFE

          LETTER RECEIVED BY LT. C.P.W. FROM A GIRL HE
          DATED TWO YEARS AGO IN FLORIDA. HE HAS
          NOT SEEN HER SINCE, NOR WRITTEN TO HER.
DARLING
     I AM GOING TO SPEND THE SUMMER WITH YOUR
FOLKS. THEY ARE FINE AND ALL YOUR RELATIVES ARE
VERY KIND. ALL THE GIRLS ARE WORRYING ABOUT
THE "MAN SHORTAGE" AND BEING AN OLD MAID MAY-
BE WE CAN BEST THAT WHEN YOU GET HOME.
                        YOUR LOVING FIANCEE


DARLING
     I HAVE BEEN LIVING WITH A PRIVATE SINCE
YOU ARE GONE PLEASE DO NOT CUT OFF MY ALLOTMENT
THOUGH, AS HE DOES NOT MAKE AS MUCH MONEY AS YOU.
                    BRITISH W/O FROM WIFE


          COMPLETE LETTER
DEAR SON
     HELLO! HOW ARE YOU? WE ARE ALL WELL!
                    LOVE FROM ALL
                            DAD

Some letters received by Canadians, Yanks and British POWs from home.

John Lashley wrote this beautiful song in Stalag Luft I.
I ordered a copy of the record and still have it in my collection

# IN SOLITARY

AND SO ANOTHER DAY CREEPS BY.
ON THE WALL ANOTHER MARK.
TWILIGHT FADED FROM THE SKY.
MY LONELY CELL GROWS DARK.

A PALE MOON MAKES THE EVENING KNOWN.
THE HUSHED BIRDS SEEK THE NEST,
AND MY THOUGHTS ARE TURNING HOME
TO THE ONES I LOVE THE BEST.

THUS I MARK ANOTHER DAY.
IN THE GLOOM I BOW MY HEAD,
AND PRAY FOR LOVED ONES FAR AWAY.
THEN TURN TO MY PRISON BED.

# HITCH IN HELL

I'M SITTING HERE AND THINKING,
OF THINGS I LEFT BEHIND,
AND IT'S HARD TO PUT ON PAPER
WHAT'S RUNNING THROUGH MY MIND.

I'VE FLOWN MANY AN AIR CRAFT
AND CLEARED THOUSANDS OF MILES OF GROUND,
BUT A DREARIER PLACE THIS SIDE OF HELL
IS WAITING TO BE FOUND.

HOWEVER THERE IS ONE CONSOLATION,
SIT QUIETLY WHILE I TELL.
WHEN I DIE I'LL GO TO "HEAVEN,"
FOR I'VE DONE MY HITCH IN "HELL".

THE ANGELS WILL GREAT ME,
THE HARPS WILL START TO PLAY.
IT'S THEN YOU'LL HEAR ST PETER
SAY LOUDLY WITH A YELL,
TAKE A FRONT SEAT DEAR "MOE"
FOR YOU'VE DONE YOUR HITCH IN "HELL".

Poems written by "Kriegies."

161

# HARD TIMES OF MARCH
### (SEE PAGE 48-49 FOR GOOD TIMES)
## MARCH 16, 1945
DINNER — STEW & BOILED SPUDS

### MARCH 17
DINNER — STEW & BOILED SPUDS

### MARCH 18
DINNER — STEW & BOILED SPUDS

### MARCH 19
DINNER — STEW & BOILED SPUDS

### MARCH 20
DINNER — STEW & BOILED SPUDS

### MARCH 21
BREAKFEAST — BUTTERSOOTCH BARLEY
DINNER — STEW & BOILED SPUDS

### MARCH 22
DINNER — STEW & BOILED SPUDS

---

## GERMAN RATION CUT  MARCH-1945

|  | OLD RATION | NEW RATION |
|---|---|---|
| MEAT | 150 GR. | 120 GR. |
| FAT | 68 GR. | 35 GR. |
| POTATOES | 4500 GR. | 3360 GR. |
| BARLEY | 150 GR. | 40 GR. |
| MARGARINE | 150 GL. | 140 GR. |
| WURST | 100 GR. | 80 GR |
| SUGAR | 262.5 GR. | 140 GR. |
| CHEESE | 31 GR | 25 GR. |
| BREAD | 22.25 GR. | 1800 GR. |
| JAM | 175 GR. | 140 GL. |
| COFFEE (ERSATZ) | 35 GL. | 28 GL. |
| VEGETABLES | 500 GR. | 480 GR. |
| DRY VEGETABLES | 80 GR. | 48 GR. |
| PEAS | 100 GR. | 60 GL. |
| SALT | AS NEEDED | VERY SELDOM |
| WHITE BREAD (FOR SICK MEN IN HOSPITAL ONLY) | 300 GR. | 250 GR. |

This menu shows the starvation diet we had
in the winter and spring of HARD TIMES.
One meager meal a day and only one breakfast a week.

# 18

## Starvation Days

By February 1945, the war was taking a tremendous toll on the German forces with the American and British advancing on the west and the Russians on the eastern front. The German cities and factories, as well as their transportation system, were being destroyed.

At the prisoner-of-war camp in Eastern Germany we now wondered what would happen in the months ahead, especially since the cut in food parcel rations in January.

February started out with bad news. A half parcel came the first week and from then on, it was down hill. Our rations were cut by 70 percent throughout the month. To make matters worse, the German rations were also cut drastically. During March there were no more Red Cross parcels, and delivery of coal was cut back again. In desperation, to keep from freezing in our rooms, we cut up any wood we could find to burn. We resorted to pulling up the sub-floors, the beams in the attic, wood moldings in the bathroom and anything we could find short of making the building collapse. However, the Germans soon became aware of what we were doing and put a stop to it. We kept our clothes on 24 hours a day, sleeping as best we could with just thin blankets to cover us.

I don't remember having shots at any previous time, but during the worst starvation period, we were given typhoid shots. They were given once a week for three weeks starting March 11.

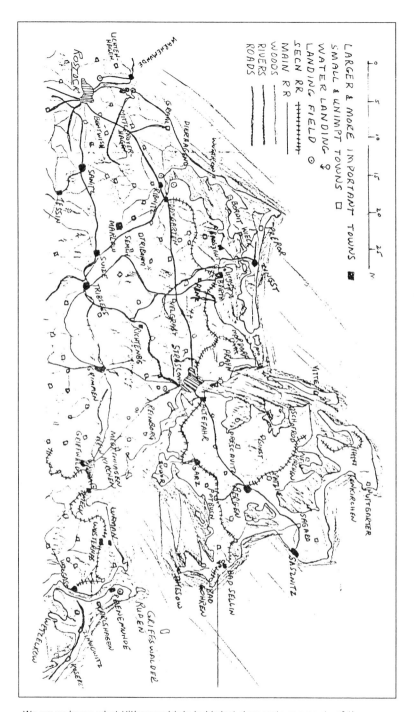

We never knew what Hitler would do in his last desperate moments of the war.
I had made this four color map in case we made a mass break out and
scattered in the countryside. I would know where I was going.

At the same time, we had to start eating out of the central dining area. We each received our reduced ration of bread and in the dining area, one meal daily of barley or watered stew with potatoes. This arrangement was in order to conserve our energy as well as the coal needed to cook our meals.

In our room I still sliced a loaf of bread very thin for all of us – this was more important than ever. One or two thin slices of bread for each of us was all we had for breakfast, evening meal, and at 9:00 p.m. The one meal in the central dining room was at midday. Otherwise, there was just enough margarine or ersatz jam to spread thinly on the bread to make it seem like a meal.

It was difficult rationing ourselves to the slices of bread during the day as we were always ravenous. One evening at 9:00 when we all began our last "meal" of the day, one of the men, Lt. Arthur "Red" Carmell, had been unable to save any of his slices through the day. He was "dying" of hunger, and I couldn't resist sharing my last slice with him.

Food had become the overriding topic of conversation in prison camp. It was very seldom that the talk turned to women and sex. We talked about our wives and families, but the all-encompassing theme was always food. On the occasions when we had received our normal Red Cross weekly package as well as bread and potatoes from the Germans, the discussion was not as tense, but as soon as the rations were cut and the parcels held up, food was the main topic.

One of the diversions was to list all the places my buddies and I could remember where we had enjoyed good meals back home. In my log I wrote about the recommendations of the other men. In Boston, it was steak at Dinty Moore's and ice cream at Thompson's Bar. In Albany, N.Y., good Italian food at Pannetta's. Ivey's in Minneapolis had the best French food, and Jim's BBQ, the best barbecue around. In Los Angeles, the recommendations were Mike Lyman's and Tail O' the Cock, and Laury's for prime rib, and Brown's in Hollywood for the best hot fudge sundae.

But New York won hands down for good memories. There was White Turkey Town House and their chicken pot pie speciality. At the Palms, 46th Street and Second Avenue, was an Italian steak joint hangout for news cartoonists. The Hunt Room at the Astor Hotel had delicious game in season, especially pheasant, and never pass up Manny Wolf's steak house at 49th and Third Avenue for a porterhouse with french fried onions for $1.50. Up at Luchow's on Times Square, there was great steak, and another winner was the Francisco Tavern, an 18th century restaurant that had delicious Lobster Newburg. Watch out for John's, an Italian restaurant, because the portions were tremendous.

But back to reality at the camp – barley, which was one of the main German rations, was a problem because it was usually full of worms. We had an argument about the etiquette of handling this problem. I agreed to get the answer for us. I wrote to Miss Emily Post, in care of the New York Daily Mirror:

"Dear Miss Post, I am a POW in Germany. One of the main foods the Germans give us is barley. Often, due to the season, of course, we find large worms in the barley. I would like to find the correct way of disposing of said worms. Some say to go ahead and eat them rapidly. If I do this, I always vomit. Others say to place them nonchalantly by the side of the bowl, but then everyone else vomits. Please set me straight." Signed, M. Kaufman, Stalag Luft I.

I never did receive an answer, and as time went on, I learned to eat the worms. They supplied needed protein in my diet.

Back in October, many of the men had thought the war would be over by Christmas. There had been no plans for the future. But here it was March and with no Red Cross parcels, and we were living on broat, barley and potatoes, and not much of that.

In the Red Cross parcels, they had included a sheet called "cultural instructions" along with packets of seeds. There was detailed information on when to plant and how to plant seeds and what we could expect to reap for our efforts. In the spring, we planted beets, carrots, tomatoes, and sweet corn. But like when one buys insurance, we hoped we wouldn't be there long enough to see them come to fruition.

In those last months of the war, the men who had something to sell, like mementos of Stalag Luft I after the war was over, were taking orders. Colonel Greening, an outstanding artist, was selling a book called "Not as Brief" for $7 to $10. Colonel Greening had flown a B-25 in Doolittle's raid on Tokyo. Later, he was shot down in Europe and had been in the underground for six months before being captured and sent to this camp. Records of songs written by "Kriegies" also were being sold. I ordered "Low Is the Sun" by John Lashley, and "All Through the Night" by Harry Korger. A story, "Behind Barbed Wire" was written by Morris J. Roy, and from Lt. K. C. Reimer came a small pamphlet of drawings of a sad story. Don Ross, who had drawn several pictures in my log book, sold a cartoon of "Klim Kriegie." All

Lt. Charlie Hecht my roommate cooking outside on a nice day.

of these were to be mementos of our experiences. I also ordered 300 photos at one cent each, but it turned out to be only 22 pictures, but they were perfect shots. One of the pictures, taken in the North 2 Compound, showed the work detail distributing Red Cross food parcels. It wasn't until recently when I looked at the photo that I recognized one of the men as myself. I don't remember posing for the photo, and I don't re-

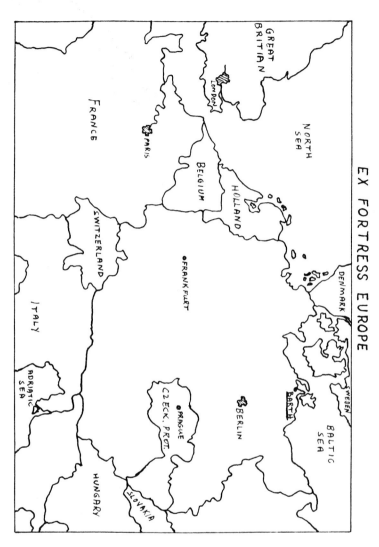

I gave Hitler's "Fortress Europe" a new name,
"EX FORTRESS EUROPE." We were at Stalag Luft I,
Barth as far north in Germany as we could be.

member recognizing myself when I received the pictures in 1945.

In addition to writing, composing, and taking pictures, some of the outstanding fighter pilots gave lectures of their experiences. On the first day I moved into Compound 2, Colonel Zemke gave a lecture called "Fighters on the Western Front." Later, Major Maniur gave a wonderful talk titled "Paratrooper over Marseilles."

In the spring of 1945, the Germans put out a bulletin with a red border, which read: "To all prisoners of war. It is no longer a sport to escape from prison camp." They told us they were setting aside certain areas of Germany which would be considered "death zones" and any escaping prisoners entering these zones would be shot on sight immediately.

But by the end of March we could sense the war was coming to an end, and the Germans started delivering our Red Cross parcels again, one a week, as before. We also were getting our Pow Wow news letter every night, and it was very exciting reading

April 1945 and many Kriegies were digging a fox hole just in case we were caught in the middle of a German/Russian battlefield.

The war is over. Shaving off the beards and planning to go home.

the reports of British, American, and Russian forces closing in on Berlin.

We had seen thousands of POWs come to our Stalag after marching across Germany ahead of the advancing Allies. By now our camp had increased to 9,000 men. There was no doubt in our minds that it would be the Russians coming from the East who would free us. In my Wartime Log, many months earlier, I had printed a full page in block letters: "Kriegie War Cry – Come on Joe," referring to Joseph Stalin.

Though there certainly were hardships, there never had been a moment of despair for me in my entire period as a POW. From the moment I was captured, I had known the Germans were on the run. The first five months of trials and tribulations after I was shot down had been a time of hardship, but also of making new friends. When Christmas came, I had been given a big lift by receiving my first letter from home, and the knowledge that

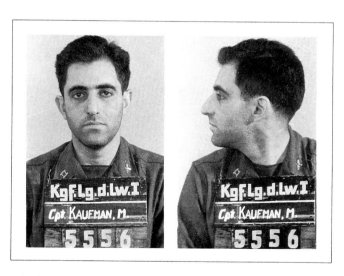

The first thing I did when the Germans evacuated and even before the Russians came in, I ransacked the Germans' office and took my personal records. I even took the negative of my mug shot.

my family knew I was alive and well. Christmas food parcels also helped make that a perfect day. Even the starvation diet of February and March did not beat me down because I knew that American and British troops were fighting on German soil. So there never was a time for me to feel despair, just the realization we were winning the war.

In the last few days of April, everything seemed to be coming to a head. The German commandant met with Colonel Zemke and the British senior officer, Group Captain Weir. The German officer had received orders that the entire camp would move to the west. But Colonel Zemke replied that under no condition would he allow his men to march out. The commandant then made his decision. He would evacuate and leave the Kriegies behind. At 1 p.m., on April 30, Major Steinhauer advised Colonel Zemke that the Germans had evacuated.

We were free.

# 19

## "The Russians Are Coming"

For some of the men, this was the first time in five or six years they had known freedom.

At 1:30 p.m. we had heard Germans outside of our area, blowing up installations away from the camp. On May 1 at 12:30 p.m. we came out of our barracks and took over the camp. That night at 10:25, the announcement of Hitler's death came over the radio, and we really went wild in rejoicing.

Major Braithwaite and Sergeant Corsin went scouting out to the south and southwest, trying to locate the Russians. They walked about eight miles before making the first contact. They identified themselves and were taken immediately to a Lieutenant

The Russians arrived and we cheered them on.

Karmyzoff. When the first Russians arrived at Stalag Luft I, Colonel Zemke and Captain Weir were at the main gate to greet them. Soon after this, drinks were flowing freely.

```
HEADQUARTERS, PROVISIONAL WING X, U. S. AAF        L.L., 000
        Stalag Luft 1, (Barth, Germany)


                                          2 May 1945


            MILITARY DISTRICT REGULATIONS
            --------------------------------

        Effective Wednesday, 2 May 1945, this district is under
   Martial Law as established by the Senior Russian Officer, Colonel
   Zchervyniok.. All personnel will comply with these district
   regulations. Failure to do so may result in being shot without
   trial,


        a) Ninety (90) men from this camp are permitted in the
           Barth area between the hours of 1000 and 2100.

        b) No man is permitted out of the camp without a pass
           obtainable only at Wing Headquarters.

        c) All passes previously issued are hereby rescinded.

        d) The official language with Russians is Russian.

        e) Personnel will obey all orders issued by Russians.

        f) All messages outgoing from this camp will be transmitted
           through the Russian Commander via Wing Headquarters,


              By order of the Commanding Officer:


                                    MARK E. HUBBARD,
                                    Lt. Col., U.S., Air Corps,
                                    Asst. Chief of Staff.

   DIST:
      1 copy ea Provisional Sqn
      2 copies ea Prov Gp
      2 copies ea RAF
      2 copies ea Hospital
      2 copies ea file
```

When the Russians arrived they set the rules. Without this
some POWs could have been hurt or killed roaming the countryside.

The "Kriegies" had managed to fix the radio so that they could connect it to loud speakers, and we listened to the Lucky Strike Hit Parade broadcast from the BBC in London.

For the next couple of days we did nothing but celebrate. The barn where the Red Cross parcels had been stored was opened up and the packages were distributed. For the first time, we had all the food we wanted. The Russians rounded up cattle and slaughtered them, and barbecues were set up in all the compounds. We feasted on meat and potatoes, and soon the starvation of February and March was forgotten.

Then trouble began. Zemke and the top command of the camp started negotiating with the Russians for permission to fly us out to France. We were concerned that the Russians would decide to march us the thousand miles to Odessa on the Black Sea. There was no way that these 9,000 "Kriegies" in their weakened condition could survive even 50 miles. But on May 7, we went wild again, tearing down the fences and raising hell the rest of the day.

It was a very special occasion to have four Russian soldiers visit us one night and share food with us – there were two captains, one lieutenant, and one technician. We had a wonderful time getting drunk. I don't remember where the liquor came from, but we had a ball. It was hard to believe that a bunch of Americans who spoke no Russian and a group of Russians who spoke no English could have such a great time. I asked the four of them to write messages in my log, and when I got home, I had the messages translated. They all said approximately the same thing:

"To the comrades in arms in a joint struggle from fascists … from Officer Drosdov Sergei, 12 May 1945. Town of Barth, Germany."

Another one was, "Americans are good friends and they proved it during the period of 1941 to 1945. I'm writing these few words to express my friendship and respect to my comrade in joint fight with Hitler and Germany and in joint victory over

Товарищу по совместной
борьбе с ~~[зачёркнуто]~~ гитлеровской
Германией — от русского офицера капитана Слер Генриха —
12 мая 1945 г. — гор. Барт
Германия

Товарищам по оружию по
совместной борьбе с фашист-
ской нечистью от русского
офицера лейтенанта Дроздова
Сергея. 12 мая 1945года г. Барт
Германия

Американцы хорошие друзья
и доказали это в период 1941-45г.г.
В знак уважения и дружбы пишу
эти несколько слов Соратнику по раз-
грому гитлеровской Германии
Капитан Мерешинский Евгений
12. мая 1945года [подпись]

Товарищам по оружию в борьбе
с нацистской тиранией в войне
1941 - 1945г.
Техник Шкулипа
12. 05. 45г.

Four Russians joined us for food and drinks in our room one night.
They wrote their feelings for us, comrades in the fight against Hitler.

it." Signed, Capt. Mereshinsky Evgeny. Dated 12 May 1945.

Meanwhile, Colonel Zemke had given orders that no one was to leave camp and go into town, but there were always a few who did what they pleased. One of them was my roommate, Red Carmell from Boston. Red had been shot down in a B-17 over Norway by a woman manning a flak gun. He went into Barth and came back and reported what he had seen and done. He said he saw only women, children, and very old men. All the older boys and able-bodied men had been taken into the army to fight for their Fatherland.

(Many years later, I met an American who had been in a military school in Germany in 1944. He said the Wehrmacht had come to the school and drafted students into the army. He was one even though he was only 15 years old at the time.)

Hitler in his desperation had been scraping the bottom of the barrel for manpower. The Russians, Americans, and British had captured hundreds of thousands of Germans in Africa, across Europe from Normandy, and in the rout from Stalingrad across Russia.

Red Carmell said that as he walked down the street of the town, he saw women hanging out of the windows. One beckoned to him to come in, and when he entered the house, she led him up to the bedroom. The German women knew what the German soldiers had done to the Russian women as they captured cities and towns, advancing across Russia. Having heard stories about rape and ravaging, the women were frightened of the Russians. This woman thought she could entice an American into her home, and he would protect her from the Russians. The woman took Red into her bedroom and started taking her clothes off. Red said he waited for her to lie down on the bed and then he spat on her and walked out.

This incident reminded me of what Red had told us many months earlier. He had been a bombardier on a B-17 and had worn his Jewish tallis (prayer shawl) on his combat mission. But when his plane was hit, the first thing he did was to dispose of his tallis before he bailed out over enemy territory. He did not want to be taken prisoner by the Germans with this around his shoulders.

At the same time the Russians were freeing us, they discovered a concentration camp a short distance away. The next day a two-page bulletin was distributed to all the men in the barracks, describing in detail the horrors of what had been found in the concentration camp. This turned out to be only the beginning of what the world was to learn about the inhumanity of the Nazis.

This is the bulletin we received:

BARTH CONCENTRATION CAMP

Three hundred slave prisoners were liberated on May 1 by the advancing Russian armies. Most of these were starved and seriously ill, the remnants of an over-packed concentration camp which, but a few days before, held an estimated 4,000 men. Too weak to walk, they had been left behind when the other prisoners were evacuated by sea several days before the arrival of the Russian army.

Most of the prisoners had been evacuated from other concentration camps, both to the east and west of Barth. Hundreds had died en route. Nationalities consisted of Czechs, Russians, Poles, Greeks, Hungarians,Austrians, French, and Italians, the majority of Jewish origin.

Only a few were strong enough to be interviewed. Worst cases were sunken-eyed skeletons, covered with ulcers, filth and vermin. British and American medical officers from the Prisoners of War Camp were rushed to remove the men to a captured Luftwaffe hospital only a block away from the concentration camp.

A Czech Jewish doctor from Prague said that of the 300 that were evacuated from the Poulitz Camp near Stettin, six weeks ago, all had died either en route or after arrival at Barth. He had been in a number of concentration camps since 1941, the worst being Belsen-Bergen near Brunswick. Thousands of prisoners, he stated, had died of starvation, disease, and ill treatment or had been killed by the Germans in a gas chamber and cremated at this camp.

At Barth, as in the other concentration camps he had been at, the doctor said that prisoners were awakened at 4:30 in the morning, given one loaf of bread for eight men for breakfast, and sent out to work in German factories, railroads, and fields until 8:00 at night. They were given no food during the day and upon their return at night to the camp, were given a small bowl of soup. If a man became ill and unable to work, he received no food from the Germans. Beatings and other bestialities were common occurrences in most of the camps he had been in, the doctor stated. If a man fell while working, his comrades were beaten if they tried to assist him. Each day the men went out to work, not knowing if they would live through the day.

The camp was originally intended for a small number of slave workers, but as the German armies retreated, thousands of concentration camp prisoners were brought to Barth. Double and triple-decked wooden bunks were jammed into the small cells. Each straw-covered bunk accommodated two to three men. Toilet facilities were not available after the failure of the water supply and the floors were covered with human waste and vomit. The men were forced to eat, sleep, and live in these deplorable conditions. Many were unable to get out of their filthy vermin-ridden beds.

The camp was surrounded with electrically-charged wire; the buildings were two-story brick structures, built very solidly. Prisoners were permitted no communication with the outside and French prisoners of war living only a few blocks away were unaware of the conditions. Inspecting Russian officers shook their heads as they looked at the horrible filth of the prisoners' living quarters. They remarked that they had seen much worse in Russia and Poland, where millions have died in the concentration camps.

A 15-year-old Polish Jew, six years in German concentration camps, helpless and listless, only able to stare up when questioned, does not know where his family is. Another 15-year-old Polish Jew spent eight months at the Barth camp, prior to which he had been at the Stettin camp, which was in the same condition.

One German Jew who spoke English, had been in concentration camps for six years. He is 40 years old and has the appearance of one 60. Since 1939 he had been in many camps and at all of them, beating and bestiality was prevalent. Though he is starved, he was permitted nothing to eat other than a half of a glass of milk every hour.

Only 24 of the 2,000 Greek Jews who were evacuated from the Stettin camp are still alive. En route to Barth, hundreds were beaten and left lying on the roads. One man had lived in New York City for 14 years. He returned to Greece in 1933 and served in the Greek army, fighting against the Italians for six months before being captured by the Germans. His mother, father, wife, five children, two brothers, and a sister were all taken to German concentration camps. he does not know where they are or whether they are still alive.

After receiving medical care, some of the prisoners, zombie-like in appearance, wandered aimlessly into the town of Barth. They could not seem to realize that they had been liberated, and upon seeing an Allied soldier in town, bowed in humble subservience..

At the Luftwaffe hospital, German women assisted in the care of the prisoners. They were horrified at the condition of the prisoners and although they lived but a few miles away in Barth, claimed to have no knowledge of the prevailing conditions.

When the prisoners went to work, they were shackled and guarded from conversation with anyone but armed German guards

Before the German guards evacuated, a number of the 300 prisoners left behind were beaten as a farewell gift.

The clothing worn by the prisoners consisted of thin, striped gray suits and ill-fitting flimsy coats, made of a cheap cotton fabric. The same garments were worn in the coldest weather for all outdoor work.

The prisoners were rushed out for roll calls and those struggling were beaten over the head with clubs, causing the deaths of many. The men were shot indiscriminately at the slightest provocation, working at gun point.

After reading this letter and hearing what other Americans told me what they had seen, I realized the German people felt they were innocent.

When our men went into Barth and talked to the people, those Germans were shocked to learn that this terrible concentration camp had really existed right outside of their town. They claimed the German soldiers never told any of them what they were really doing there every day. What did the German people really think when hundreds of thousands of their fellow Germans, their neighbors, were rounded up and shipped away in trucks and freight cars, never to be heard from again?

They were told that they were a superior race of people, and they believed it.

When they bombed Poland, they were told that was right, and they believed it.

In 1940 when they bombed England and the innocent cities and town, they were told that was right, and they believed it.

When the Americans and British bombed their factories and cities years later, they said we were gangsters. They not only believed this but tried and actually did kill unarmed airmen who parachuted into their midst.

How could such a "civilized" people be so right?

As our commanding officer, Col. Henry Spicer said to 1,500 POWs that early morning in November 1944, "If we stay here 15 years to beat them, it will be worth it.

PLANE NUMBER 8402   STALAG LUFT 1

| | NAME | RANK | SERIAL NUMBER |
|---|---|---|---|
| 1. | Henderson MA | 2nd Lt | O-749238 |
| 2. | Hill HH | 1st Lt | O-744311 |
| 3. | Hizenski JS | 2ndLt | O-811681 |
| 4. | Horsky AL | 2nd Lt | O-683910 |
| 5. | House LE | 2nd Lt | O-676304 |
| 6. | Huggett IW | 1st Lt | O-79182 2 |
| 7. | Hunt GS | 2nd Lt | O-380222 |
| 8. | Hustedt HJ | 2nd Lt | O-746353 |
| 9. | Jacobs JH | 2nd Lt | O-2057928 |
| 10. | Jakobe RE | 2nd Lt | O-755225 |
| 11. | Jenkins ER | 2nd Lt | O-679533 |
| 12. | Johnson RH | 2nd Lt | O-699372 |
| 13. | Johnson RW | 2nd Lt | O-680643 |
| 14. | Jolovtz AW | 1stLt | O-719085 |
| 15. | Kaplan LJ | 2nd Lt | O-683250 |
| 16. | Kast WL | F/O | T-124853 |
| 17. | Kattef AS | 2nd Lt | O-723731 |
| 18. | Katz LR | 2nd Lt | O-694560 |
| 19. | Kaufman L | Captain | O-728677 |
| 20. | Kaufman PP | F/O | T-2519 |
| 21. | Kehrer AR | 1st Lt | O-386193 |
| 22. | Kirkorian AG | 2nd Lt | O-684170 |
| 23. | Kirkwood SM | 2nd Lt | O-679630 |
| 24. | Kirsch J | 2nd Lt | O-1692929 |
| 25. | Kirwan TE | 2nd Lt | O-745114 |
| 26. | Klarsfeld LA | F/O | T-127713 |
| 27. | Kleinburg JE | 2nd LT | O-678377 |
| 28. | Kuptstow A | 2nd Lt | O-710276 |
| 29. | Lander LB | 1st Lt | O-825204 |
| 30. | Landsman J | 1st Lt | O-718187 |

This was my Group #8402.  May 13, 1945 we marched to Barth's
Luftwaffe Field to board the B17 on the first leg of our journey home.

# 20

## Going Home

Colonel Zemke had served with the Russians in Moscow, and he understood them and they knew they were dealing with a man who had dealt with them in the past. They continued to drink toasts to the destruction of Germany and to the great friendship among the Russians, the Americans, and the British, but their toasts and bravado did not ring true. They seemed to say one thing and do another.

It was at this moment I realized that the war was not over. Little did I know that the next war already had begun.

(One year later, on May 6, 1946 at Westminster College in Fulton, Mo., Winston Churchill called this the start of the Cold War with the Russians. The Iron Curtain had descended across the continent.)

When I returned home, none of my friends could understand what I was talking about when I said, "The war is over with the Russian people but not with the Russian leaders."

Finally, after what seemed a lifetime, the Russians agreed to allow Americans to fly in and evacuate us out of the camps.

On May 12 we finally were scheduled to move out. Six other men and I in Block 8 were chosen as leaders to form groups to fly out in the B-17s that came to get us. I was given a list of 30 officers (not "Kriegies" any more) to line up and march out to a B-17.

Our turn came on May 13 when we actually walked out to the plane and loaded up. This was the day we had been waiting for.

As we were boarding, some of the guys kissed the planes and said, "This is American. This is home."

As we took off and circled, we looked down to see Stalag Luft I for the last time. I went up to the cockpit and talked to the pilot and copilot.I had a nice long conversation about what had been going on in the last month of the war in Europe, and they were interested in what had happened to us.

In the plane, plywood had been placed over the bomb bays in order to give us as much room as possible. Pretty soon the pilot began flying low, skimming 50 feet over the valleys and hills of the countryside. As a pilot of a bomber, he had not had the chance to fly so low. I didn't tell him that for me, a fighter pilot, 50 feet was not very low.

Before we knew it, we had landed at Rheims, France, where we spent the first night.

Within a few days, this city would be the location of the meeting between the German and Allied High Command, to sign the final surrender of Hitler's Germany, the end of World War II in Europe.

The next day we moved to St. Valerie and Camp Lucky Strike, a tent city that looked like it had been put together in a hurry in order to house the 80,000 to 90,000 men who were arriving from POW camps all over Europe. It was crude but the camps seemed a haven to me. There was plenty of food with lots of meat and potatoes to fatten us up before we went home. Pretty Red Cross ladies were out in full force handing out candy, chewing gum, and other refreshments, but best of all, they were friendly females to talk to.

There were tents for social gatherings, places where we could relax, read, and talk. Any help we needed, they were there to assist us.

I don't know how it happened, but I ended up with a Jeep, and I still had my love of exploring the countryside. I had heard that the Catholic Benedictine Order had a place near our camp where they made and bottled their famous Benedictine liqueur. It was not hard to find the place, and I went into the small building at the front that served as a show room. I asked to buy two bottles of Benedictine, and they said they would be glad to sell me the liqueur but I would have to provide empty bottles because of a shortage.

I solved this problem quickly by getting into my Jeep and driving around to the back of the plant where there were bottles that had been turned in. I helped myself to two empties, drove back around to the front and handed in the bottles in exchange for two full one. I also bought a dozen of the little one-shot souvenir bottles. As I recall, I didn't feel the least bit guilty. After all, all's fair in love and war.

When I returned to the camp, I shared one of the bottles with my comrades, and packed up the other plus the 12 souvenir bottles to take home. ("Later I opened the box at my mother's apartment in New York and took out the large bottle plus a small one as a gift for the family. The next morning I discovered my

POWs going home on the Admiral Mayo.

mother had tossed out what she thought was a box of crumpled up newspapers and had sent the 11 souvenir bottles of Benedictine down the garbage chute.")

On June 14, exactly a month and a half after Hitler's death, I boarded the transport ship Admiral Mayo at LeHavre, France. Victor Mature, the Hollywood movie star, was a sailor on the ship and he visited us in our cabin. He was very interested in hearing about our experiences in prison camp.

It was a pleasant cruise across the Atlantic – the last time for me to be with my close friends with whom I had shared so much.

We saw Boston on the horizon – just as welcoming a sight as the Statue of Liberty, and steamed into the harbor. As we pulled up to the dock, we were welcomed in style by a large crowd and an army band. It brought tears of joy to my eyes.

For us, the war was over.

Right: Sailing home on the Admiral Mayo. Sitting on the right in a lounge chair.
Left: In Boston looking down from the deck of the troop transport
Admiral Mayo at the welcoming band.

# 6000 U. S. FLIERS FREED BY REDS AT BALTIC PORT

## American Ace Put in Charge Of Prison Camp by Germans Who Fled on Hearing That Russians Were Coming

By the Associated Press.

LUNEBERG, Germany, May 11.— Six thousand American fliers have been liberated by the Russians at Barth on the Baltic, where the fleeing Germans left their prison camp in charge of the Missoula, Mont., ace, Col. Hubert C. Zemke.

The fliers at Stalagluft had awaited the arrival of the Russians. Their German guards had fled. Besides the Americans, 300 RAF fliers were liberated.

Col. Zemke was commander of the top-scoring 56th Thunderbolt Group and had been missing since Fall when his fighter plane was destroyed. Two weeks ago a German officer approached him and said:

"We are all leaving. The Russians are coming. The camp is in your hands."

Airmen, armed with clubs, were ordered by Col. Zemke to guard the camp, which is directly north of Berlin. Another detachment went to a nearby airfield to dig out mines and prevent the Germans from wrecking it. Guards were posted around the camp to keep panicked civilians from entering it in their flight from the Russians.

The story was pieced together today by Maj. W. P. Lightfoot of Des Moines, Ia., American contact officer for prisoners of war at this clearing center of Luneberg. Maj. Lightfoot questioned 300 American fliers who left Stalagluft 1 and made their way to Luneberg. They were flown from here to Le Havre for embarkation to the British Isles.

These 100 officers and 200 enlisted men left the camp by a "back door" although Col. Zemke was trying to enforce order and have the men remain for evacuation by the Russians, according to a Supreme Headquarters directive.

The men who sneaked out said they took the chance of getting back to British territory, rather than awaiting evacuation by the Russians through Odessa, a process that probably would take several months.

Some left camp on small boats and crossed 60 miles of open water for Sweden, the escaped men said. Lieut. Col. Frank Eresch of Topeka, Kan., is here waiting permission to go to the camp and help arrange details of the evacuation.

---

The story of the liberation of 6,000 fliers at Stalag Luft I.

I'm on the high seas only hours away from America.

# Nazi Camp Held Galaxy of U.S. Aces

## Zemke and Gabreski Among Yank Fliers Found at Barth

**By Andy Rooney**
Stars and Stripes Staff Writer

The greatest collection of American air aces ever assembled sat, some of them for a year and a half, in Stalagluft I, the German prison camp at Barth on the Baltic, before they were freed.

The camp was under the command of Col. Hubert Zemke, the Missoula, Mont. ace, whose 56th Fighter Group made the P47 famous. With Zemke were five other former fighter group commanders, all colonels, a full squadron of aces headed by Lt. Col. Francis S. Gabreski, of Oil City, Pa., who holds the all-time American record for German planes shot down with 28 to his credit, and approximately 1,000 other American P51, P47 and P38 pilots

Among the best known aces at the camp were Majors Jerry Johnson, who destroyed 16 German planes before he went down, and Duane Beeson, who knocked down 18.

### Few Shot Down by Luftwaffe

Few of the U.S. aces found their Luftwaffe superiors in actual air combat, but were forced down after being hit with flak on low-level strafing or bombing missions.

The 26-year-old Gabreski had a strange accident which forced him to land in Germany on July 20, 1944.

"We had been escorting bombers," Gabreski said, "and were on the way home when we strafed an airdrome near Coblenz. I was overshooting a plane on the ground. I stuck the nose down a little to get on the target and the propellor hit the ground. Oil sprayed all over my windshield and canopy. The engine was failing so I set the plane on the ground at about 200 miles an hour. It finally stopped and I got out and left it burning."

### Captured After Five Days

Gabreski escaped capture for five days but finally was trapped, exhausted and hungry, by German farmers and was turned over to the Wehrmacht. He was taken to the Luftwaffe interrogation center at Dulag Luft.

"There was an interrogator there we called Stone Face Scharff," Gabreski said.

"As I opened the door and walked in the first day, he said: 'Why

**Col. Hubert Zemke**

Gabreski! We've been expecting you for a long time. Glad to see you'."

The Germans were familiar with most of the American air aces by name, reputation and ability to outfly Luftwaffe pilots, long before they fell into their hands. German radio frequently warned the 56th Fighter Group that "the Luftwaffe is laying for Zemke's Wolfpack."

### Put in Solitary Confinement

When Zemke, one of the most colorful figures in the air force despite his reticence about publicity, was forced down, he was interrogated in a routine manner and started for a prison camp. While he was en route, German headquarters apparently came across the "Zemke" file and simultaneously a public relations information sheet was issued from Washington which stated, among other things, that Zemke had served in liaison capacity with the Russians when the U.S. first started shipping planes to Russia. Zemke's trip was interrupted, he was clapped into solitary confinement and interrogated steadily for several weeks.

The former fighter group commanders at the Barth prison camp included Col. Einar Malmstrom, of Spokane, Wash. (356th Fighter Group), Col. Henry R. Spicer, of San Antonio, Texas (357th Fighter Group), Lt. Col. Glenn Duncan and Lt. Col. Loren G McCollom, of Ritzville, Wash., both of whom did

### Flak, Not Luftwaffe, Forced Down Most Of the Airmen

pioneer work with their fighter group experimenting with the P47 as a dive bomber. They led the first attacks in which 500-pound bombs were dropped from wing racks on P47s.

**Food Was Biggest Worry**

The fighter pilots confined at Barth, many of whom now are in Paris working on the evacuation of other prisoners or waiting to return to the States, said that their greatest worry at Barth was food.

The Germans gave them a loaf of bread a day to be split among seven men. They also got a bowl of dishwater stew concocted from turnips and an occasional slice of potato.

Sometimes, after a spell of cold weather when the streets were slippery with ice, or following days of American strafing attacks on roads cluttered with horse-drawn carts, the prisoners were given horsemeat as a special treat.

Prisoners defined the difference between good and bad mess sergeants thus: "A good mess manager would tell you there were worms in the food. A bad mess manager wouldn't tell you."

### Gabreski Anxious to Pit Skill Against Japanese

NEW YORK, May 25 (ANS).— Lt. Col. Francis S. Gabreski, Eighth AF ace who knocked down 28 German planes before being forced down himself nearly a year ago, reported to the War Department at Washington yesterday before starting a 60-day leave.

He said he "definitely" wants to get into the Pacific war. "In fact," he declared, "all those men I talked to in the prison camp were anxious to go there. Give those men 30 days' leave and they'll be just as good as new again and ready to tackle the Japs."

Gabreski said he will spend part of his leave with his parents in Oil City, Pa., but indicated that he might get married to his fiancee, Kay Cochrane, of Prairie du Chien, Wis., whom he hasn't seen since October, 1942, a month before he left for the ETO.

Miss Cochrane told reporters there would be no wedding plans until she talked the whole thing over with him.

Col. Hubert Zemke telling how it was.

# Hitler Wanted to Kill All PWs

The Swiss Radio confirmed yesterday reports that in the last days of the war Adolf Hitler ordered all Allied prisoners of war shot.

Heard by BBC in London, the radio quoted Dr. Burckhardt, president of the International Red Cross. He said that the Wehrmacht had refused to carry out the order and that in March he had met representatives of Heinrich Himmler and obtained permission for the Red Cross to enter PW camps and prevent any last-minute executions.

Last March, at the time of Dr. Burckhardt's visit to Germany, reports that Allied prisoners in Germany would be killed were widespread, but Himmler was blamed at that time. The reports never were officially recognized because of Allied concern over what might happen if Burckhardt's mission were a failure.

Dr. Burckhardt also said that Hitler always had wanted to renounce the international conventions relating to prisoners of war, and that toward the last days of his life, his temper steadily grew worse.

This story tells why we made escape maps with a mad man like Hitler calling the shots.

# Epilogue

In June 1949 I was flying at Hamilton Field in the reserves with the 73rd Fighter Squadron on two weeks active duty. I had heard that our personal files had been moved from Utah to this base, and I was very curious about what was in my file concerning my bailing out of the P-39 at this same field in October 1942. When I went to a captain in the file section at the base, he found my file and the first thing he noticed was that I was the wrong rank, according to the papers. He said I should have been promoted to major in 1945 when I was still on active duty. I replied that I had received a copy of an order that denied me this promotion. The captain said this was an error and could be corrected in five minutes. However, after I completed my two weeks on active duty at major's pay, I would have to leave my outfit because there was not room in it for another major. I decided to take the promotion and a few minutes later I was at the PX buying my new gold leaves. When I reported to the ready room with the insignia of my new rank, I really set off a mad rush among the other men for the record section and one second lieutenant got bumped up to first lieutenant as a result.

However, the real spin-off from the strange promotion was the following year when the entire squadron from captain down was recalled to active duty and sent to Korea. They didn't need more majors and so I was able to stay home with my wife and two children. I had suffered with a bad back since 1945 and I knew that if I ever was recalled to active duty, I would have to admit to this problem, but in the meantime, I had enjoyed flying trainers on weekends at a base just 15 minutes from my home.

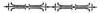

In 1954 I received a call from my mother in New York City saying she had had a midnight call from a family friend, a former Air Force man. He told her he had just returned from an Army Air Corps reunion at the Biltmore Hotel, where one of the guest speakers had been Hanns Scharff. It seems Scharff had been brought to this country to testify in the trial of an American who had collaborated with Germany during the war.

Hanns Scharff, of course, was the man who had interrogated me and numerous other Air Force officers who had been shot down and taken to Dulag Luft near Frankfurt. He was considered one of Germany's leading interrogators. In his talk he had referred to three officers with whom the German interrogators had had no success. The third officer he mentioned was Capt. Mozart Kaufman, and he told the group some of the subterfuges he had used to try to get information from Kaufman about his outfit and other matters. My mother remembered my telling her about some of these experiences.

It was after this call that I realized Hanns Scharff really didn't have the information about me that he wanted. Even though at the end of the month in solitary confinement, he told me he knew all about my unit, the information was old by the time he had received it. It made me feel very good to know my refusal to cooperate and to keep my mouth shut in solitary had been worthwhile.

In 1958 I made my first trip to Europe since the war. In Paris I was determined to find the railroad station where I had been held captive for several days with 59 fellow prisoners. My lack of knowledge of French except for a few polite expressions did not make it easy, but I finally learned that the Gare du Nord, the railroad station for trains to the north, was the one for trains to Frankfurt, Germany. I took a taxi to the station and walked through the large entrance with very mixed emotional feelings. As I walked through the long area where trains arrived and departed, memories flooded back to me. I turned left and walked down to the end, finding my way as if I had been there yesterday. There, up to the left on the second floor were the round half windows. I stopped, not believing I could be back in this same place again. I walked up the stairs and went right to the room where I had been brought as a POW and had lived for a short period of my life. I stood in the open doorway expecting to see army cots lined up, but instead, there were rows of desks with office workers at them. I stood there fascinated, unable to move, until someone came up to ask if I could be helped. All I could do was to say no thank you in my poor French. I turned and went around the corner and into the men's toilet, where the room and walls were as old and dirty looking as the day I had left for Frankfurt.

Then I went downstairs, turned right and started slowly down toward the other end of the station, seeing in my mind the German soldiers and their families milling around me, rushing to leave Paris. I opened my eyes, and this was a French railroad station in 1958, not August 9, 1944, and there was no German guard escorting me through the crowded building.

Halfway down, I saw a round glass lighted sign with a green cross on it – my first aid station. I went there and walked slowly through the door, seeing a nurse with her stiff white cap on her head and the table with the pointed-top bottles, which had held alcohol. The nurse asked if she could help me, and I tried to explain to her that I had been here in 1944. She became very excited and took me by the arm to lead me to an interpreter. After explaining to him my experience in 1944, the nurse became very excited and said that the same nurse who had taken care of me still worked there, but this was her day off. I told the nurse to give a message of thanks to the one who had helped an American pilot and to let her know how much those plums had meant to me. We parted after many "mercis." I went out into the sunshine of Paris to resume my post-war life.

In 1973, 30 years later, driving through Normandy my wife and I visited villages where I had been stationed. We tried to find some traces of the old field near Deux-Jumeaux but all we found were sections of the steel matting layed down for our landing strip. The farmers had used them to make fences around their properties. The traces of war had vanished from this small section of France.

Driving through the villages, we saw small memorials with fresh flowers by the side of the road commemorating American privates or sergeants or officers who had been the first to liberate the villages from the oppression of four years of Nazi rule. These American men, many no more than boys, had crossed the ocean to fight and make France free again.

It was 1979, and by this time, my wife and I had begun importing fine English and French antiques for our retail operation. On one of our buying trips we drove down to Ringwood and then over to Ibsley to search for my air base of 1944. Finally, behind a high fence and a massive gate, we located the buildings in which we had lived. There were several still standing but in very run-down condition. One had a sagging door with worn and weathered letters that said, "Officers and crews only." I went inside, and as memories flooded in on me, the firewood stored on the floor suddenly vanished, and I saw my friends standing there preparing for another sweep over the channel. I could see the fireplace at the far end blazing away, keeping us warm against the cold damp fog that was just beginning to dissipate. I stepped outside into the sunshine, and it still seemed like 1944. As I stood there, I realized my wife was walking away to leave me alone with my buddies of long ago. I didn't move for about 20 minutes,

In 1979 we located the old air field at Ibsley.
This is what was left of the door for Officers and Crews – "icers and rews."

In 1979, the inside of this building was an old storage room.
But I still had memories of buddies sitting around the fireplace in 1944.

dreaming of the glories of those wonderful exciting times. Finally, my time with the past was up, and I returned to the present. I learned from a nearby resident that there was an old man who lived down the road who had been here during the war. I found Mr. Sampson, a very old dairy farmer in worn clothes, who told me our field had become a gravel pit and before that, a plant nursery. When the nursery was closed, Mr. Sampson had rescued daffodil bulbs that had been thrown out and planted them in a little garden in the woods. The photograph my wife took of us in this little forest garden filled with daffodils later became the scene of a painting I did of Mr. Sampson walking down a path into the sun. Mr. Sampson had made many friends of the men from our group and had wonderful memories of the Americans during that short span of history in England.

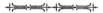

In 1979 I received a phone call from Woody Klinner Jr., my wing man on that last fateful flight. It was as if time had stood still, and we talked about the 494th Squadron as if it was yesterday. We made plans for him to visit me from his home in Alabama, and the following summer he came to San Francisco. For three days, we did nothing but talk about the past and he told me things I had not known. I had thought that a ricochet from my gunfire on the tank had set my plane on fire, but Woody said he had spotted a machine gun nest on a hill behind the tank and that's who had shot me down. He also told me that as my plane burst into flames on the deck, he had called out to me that I was on fire. At that moment, I was pulling up for a bail out. Woody also said that my plane exploded and disappeared from the sky moments after I bailed out. As Woody circled to cover me and to see if I landed safely, he also was hit by ground fire and had to bail out. He ended up with a broken rib and a punctured lung in German-occupied Rennes. No sooner was he settled in a hospital, than General Patton's tanks surrounded the area, and Woody was back in England in short order.

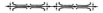

In January 1982, we had a devastating flood in San Anselmo, Calif., where I had my business. When we were cleaning up from the wreckage, another local businessman approached me and asked if I was a former prisoner of war. When I said I was, he told me he was reading a book, "The Interrogator," by Raymond Tolliver, which was about Hanns Scharff of Oberursel. In the book, there was a story about me, and how the interrogator had tried to gain information from me for one month. The story was mainly accurate but with a few of the details incorrect.

I wrote to Raymond Tolliver to compliment him on the book and to tell him about the few details that were wrong with my story. I said the errors were unimportant and that I just wanted to introduce myself to him. A month later on a Sunday morning, I received a phone call and I knew immediately who it was. But before I could say his name, he introduced himself as Hanns Scharff. We started talking, and I said to him, "You son of a bitch - I'll never forgive you for what you did to me." He asked me what it was he had done, and I told him that after keeping me in solitary confinement for 30 days, he had given me a large bowl of noodles and soup. And after I had devoured that, he had given me another one. He then sent me on my way, and from that time on, I began getting plenty of food. But I became so sick from eating all those noodles that I was unable to eat for the next week. I told him I could forgive him for keeping me in solitary confinement for a month, but I could never forgive him for making me sick with too much food just when I was about to receive full rations for the first time since I had been shot down.

Needless to say, Raymond Tolliver, Hanns Scharff, and I have been good correspondents and telephone friends since then. The author and the one-time interrogator both live in Southern California now.

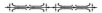

On Sept. 10, 1992, Hanns Scharff died at his home in Bear Valley Springs, Calif. He was brought to this country after the war to testify about U.S. pilots who had become traitors during the war. He returned later to become a U.S. Citizen and a renowned artist. He was especially noted for his artistic ability and went on to gain a reputation for his magnificent work in mosaics. A few of his more famous jobs were the Capital Building, Sacramento, Calif., works at Disney World, Epcot Centre and many others. Many formers POWs had met him over the years and accepted him as a friend and a fellow American. I'm proud to say that I was among them.

In April 1982 I wrote to the Air Force magazine and asked them to print a notice requesting anyone who knew the whereabouts of Col. H. R. Spicer to contact me as I had a copy of his famous speech at Stalag Luft I in 1944.

The deluge of letters from all over the nation surprised me, as more than 40 men and women wrote to me. Some told me of serving with him, others of what they had heard about him. But all the letters contained the same two elements – the first was a great admiration for the man as a leader, pilot, and individual, and the second was a desire for a copy of the speech he gave that fateful day of November 1, 1944.

Forty-seven years after I first met him in 1944, I went to see Lt. Coleman Jacobson in Dallas, Texas where he is a well-known dermatologist. He recalled seeing me walk out of my solitary cell at Dulag Luft in September 1944 and said he couldn't believe what I looked like. I was a terrible sight. I had not shaved for a month, was wearing the same clothes I was captured in and was thin after a month on a starvation diet. He said all he thought of at the time was that he hoped he was not in for the same treatment. He had been a bombardier in a B-24 and had been shot down only a few days earlier.

In November 1991, Jim Miller, the president of the Rotary Club of Ross Valley, Calif. asked me to give the invocation for the Veterans Day meeting. This is the prayer I gave:

November 11, Armistice Day, is in honor of the men and women who had died during two centuries, giving their lives to preserve the way of life that we are able to live in peace with our wives and children. For me, it reminds me of my friends and buddies I lost from Hamilton Field to the Aleutians, England, France, and Stalag Luft I. To all of them – I salute them – and thank them for what they did for me – and all of us.

# Index

## Q

Quasada, General Elwood R. "Pete", 88
Quintana, Lt. Milbern A., 85, 86

## R

Rebello, Sgt. Walt, 131
Reimer, Lt. K.C., 167
Rice, 2nd Lt. Don R., 131
Reid, Lt. Richard, 71
Robbins, Gwin, 3
Rommel, General, 70
Roney, Lt. William M., 34
Ross, Don, 132, 140, 141, 167
Roy Morris, J., 167

## S

Sampson, William R.W., 194, 195
Scharff, Hanns, 105, 109, 110, 113, 143, 146, 192, 196, 197
Sergei, Officer Drosdov, 175
Sherman, Lt. Eric H., 131, 148
Smith, Lt., 38
Snow, Cadet Kenneth, 13
Soloman, Lt. J.A., 131
Spicer, Col. Henry R., 119, 123, 126, 137, 139, 140, 141, 181, 197
Spigler, Lt., 34
Stalin, Joseph, 171
Staring, Lt. John, 55, 86, 89, 93
Stark, 2nd Lt. Richard D., 147
Steinhauer, Major, 119, 137, 147, 172
Stone, Capt. "Doc", 82

## T

Tangerman, Mr., 11, 12
Tolliver, Raymond, 107, 196, 197

## V

Van Risswick, Lt. Anton G., 95
Vevavdoski, Sgt., 42

## W

Watson, Capt. John W., 52, 84, 143
Watt, Lt. Col. James R., 40
Weir, Group Captain, 172, 174
Wertenbaker, Col. George C., 52, 70, 88
Williams, Lt. Richard, 57, 84, 89
Wilson, Lt. Col., 139, 143

## Y

Young, Lt. Robert C., 49

## Z

Zeinka, Lt. Edward, 49, 75, 93
Zemke, Col. Hubert, 146, 167, 172, 174, 175, 177, 183, 189

# Order Form

Mozart Kaufman was a WW II Fighter Pilot. After earning his wings in the Army Air Force, he had his first battle before facing the enemy. In a P-39 Aircobra fighter plane at Hamilton Field, California after five pilots were lost in practice maneuvers with no answers for the crashes, he was the first pilot to bail out and live to tell what caused the planes to crash.

Next, on to Alaska and the Aleutians and 24 combat missions against the Japanese where battling the severe weather turned out to be more threatening than the enemy. And then on to Europe and his most exciting tour of duty. Stationed in Southern England he flew his beloved P-47 Thunderbolt fighter plane, the most outstanding fighter plane of World War II, escorting bombers over Germany and France and strafing enemy ground troups.

Early morning June 6, 1944 he found himself bombing and strafing and taking part in support of Eisenhower's Normandy invasion. On his 50th mission on July 30, he was shot out of the sky while bombing German tanks in ground level attacks. Bailing out of a flaming plane at 500 feet, he was captured and relentlessly interrogated in solitary confinement for 30 days. He finally ended up in Stalag Luft I. His experiences of his 10 months in prison camp under the rigors of one of the coldest winters on record, the deprivation of food, and death threats are the highlights of this book.

There are 224 pages with over 90 photographs (most of which he personally took) and amusing drawings taken from his POW scrapbook. This exciting story is told with candor, sensitivity, and a sense of humor, taking the reader along on some of the most daring and thrilling escapades of one's life.

---

Send me _____ copies @ $12.95 each                                    _____
Shipping & handling $2.00 (add 75¢ for each additional book)            _____
California residents add 7.25% tax                                      _____
Enclose check or money order, made payable to MOZART KAUFMAN           _____

Name _____

Address _____

City, State, Zip _____

Phone _____

**Send to: Mozart Kaufman, 2 Magnolia Avenue, San Anselmo, CA 94960**

# Order Form

Mozart Kaufman was a WW II Fighter Pilot. After earning his wings in the Army Air Force, he had his first battle before facing the enemy. In a P-39 Aircobra fighter plane at Hamilton Field, California after five pilots were lost in practice maneuvers with no answers for the crashes, he was the first pilot to bail out and live to tell what caused the planes to crash.

Next, on to Alaska and the Aleutians and 24 combat missions against the Japanese where battling the severe weather turned out to be more threatening than the enemy. And then on to Europe and his most exciting tour of duty. Stationed in Southern England he flew his beloved P-47 Thunderbolt fighter plane, the most outstanding fighter plane of World War II, escorting bombers over Germany and France and strafing enemy ground troups.

Early morning June 6, 1944 he found himself bombing and strafing and taking part in support of Eisenhower's Normandy invasion. On his 50th mission on July 30, he was shot out of the sky while bombing German tanks in ground level attacks. Bailing out of a flaming plane at 500 feet, he was captured and relentlessly interrogated in solitary confinement for 30 days. He finally ended up in Stalag Luft I. His experiences of his 10 months in prison camp under the rigors of one of the coldest winters on record, the deprivation of food, and death threats are the highlights of this book.

There are 224 pages with over 90 photographs (most of which he personally took) and amusing drawings taken from his POW scrapbook. This exciting story is told with candor, sensitivity, and a sense of humor, taking the reader along on some of the most daring and thrilling escapades of one's life.

---

Send me _____ copies @ $12.95 each                    _____
Shipping & handling $2.00 (add 75¢ for each additional book)   _____
California residents add 7.25% tax                        _____
Enclose check or money order, made payable to MOZART KAUFMAN   _____

Name _____

Address _____

City, State, Zip _____

Phone _____

**Send to: Mozart Kaufman, 2 Magnolia Avenue, San Anselmo, CA 94960**

# Order Form

Mozart Kaufman was a WW II Fighter Pilot. After earning his wings in the Army Air Force, he had his first battle before facing the enemy. In a P-39 Aircobra fighter plane at Hamilton Field, California after five pilots were lost in practice maneuvers with no answers for the crashes, he was the first pilot to bail out and live to tell what caused the planes to crash.

Next, on to Alaska and the Aleutians and 24 combat missions against the Japanese where battling the severe weather turned out to be more threatening than the enemy. And then on to Europe and his most exciting tour of duty. Stationed in Southern England he flew his beloved P-47 Thunderbolt fighter plane, the most outstanding fighter plane of World War II, escorting bombers over Germany and France and strafing enemy ground troups.

Early morning June 6, 1944 he found himself bombing and strafing and taking part in support of Eisenhower's Normandy invasion. On his 50th mission on July 30, he was shot out of the sky while bombing German tanks in ground level attacks. Bailing out of a flaming plane at 500 feet, he was captured and relentlessly interrogated in solitary confinement for 30 days. He finally ended up in Stalag Luft I. His experiences of his 10 months in prison camp under the rigors of one of the coldest winters on record, the deprivation of food, and death threats are the highlights of this book.

There are 224 pages with over 90 photographs (most of which he personally took) and amusing drawings taken from his POW scrapbook. This exciting story is told with candor, sensitivity, and a sense of humor, taking the reader along on some of the most daring and thrilling escapades of one's life.

---

Send me _____ copies @ $12.95 each     _____
Shipping & handling $2.00 (add 75¢ for each additional book)     _____
California residents add 7.25% tax     _____
Enclose check or money order, made payable to MOZART KAUFMAN     _____

Name _____

Address _____

City, State, Zip _____

Phone _____

**Send to: Mozart Kaufman, 2 Magnolia Avenue, San Anselmo, CA 94960**